RECONNECTING WITH NATURE: NEW HISTORIES

RIVER, SOCIETY AND CULTURE

RECONNECTING WITH NATURE
NEW HISTORIES

JADAVPUR UNIVERSITY
HISTORY MONOGRAPH SERIES

Other titles in this series:

Indian Medicinal Plants in the Shifting Terrains of Science: Botanical and Medical Literature of Nineteenth-century Bengal
NUPUR DASGUPTA

Rethinking Human–Animal Relationship: Reading Stories from Bengali Literature
ANURADHA ROY

The Gasping City: An Environmental History of Calcutta, 1817–1923
MAHUA SARKAR

RECONNECTING WITH NATURE: NEW HISTORIES

River, Society and Culture

ENVIRONMENTAL PERSPECTIVES ON THE RIVERS OF ASSAM AND BENGAL

Rup Kumar Barman

PRIMUS BOOKS
An imprint of Ratna Sagar P. Ltd.
Virat Bhavan
Mukherjee Nagar Commercial Complex
Delhi 110 009

Offices at CHENNAI LUCKNOW AGRA AHMEDABAD BENGALURU BHOPAL COIMBATORE DEHRADUN GUWAHATI HYDERABAD JAIPUR JALANDHAR KANPUR KOCHI KOLKATA MUMBAI PATNA RANCHI VARANASI

First published 2023

ISBN: 978-93-5687-835-8 (Paperback)
ISBN: 978-93-5687-052-9 (POD)

Published by Primus Books

Laser typeset by Jojy Philip
jojyphilip@gmail.com

Contents

Tables

Foreword

The research programme on environmental history of South Asia was initiated in the Department of History, Jadavpur University, under the University Grants Commission's Special Assistance Programme (SAP) in 2004. I had the privilege to head the programme during its first two phases. This programme was the first of its kind in the country. This centre for environmental history gradually earned recognition both within the country and beyond. The faculty members of the department have already published quite an impressive number of books and articles on the subject. Such publications grew out of the several SAP-funded research projects undertaken at our centre. A large number of international and national conferences, on various themes of environmental history, were organized and the department also hosted about twenty outstanding scholars in the field as visiting professors. I have already mentioned in my edited volumes *Situating Environmental History* (2007, new edn., 2021) and *Critical Themes in Environmental History of India* (2020) and in my recent monograph, *Climate, Calamity and the Wild* (Primus Books, 2022) that though environmental history is one of the most important areas of enquiry in the field of history, it still remains as a less explored field without well-defined disciplinary standards and methodological strategies. It is felt that professional historians with the requisite methodological training will be able to (a) develop and define the agenda and disciplinary canons of this field of inquiry, and (b) historicize the present-day concerns and anxieties in the broad area of environmental history.

In his recent book *The Climate of History in a Planetary Age* (Primus Books, 2021), Dipesh Chakrabarty argues that historians need to revise many of their fundamental assumptions and methodologies in this period of human-induced climate change. While confronting environmental issues today, when globalization has triggered the threat of global warming and mass extinction, historians are inventing new conceptual categories to integrate questions that they have usually treated in the past as separate and virtually unconnected. This finds manifestation in the recent rise of the term 'environmental humanities'. It is an interdisciplinary umbrella category that accommodates environmental history, environmental philosophy, cultural geography, ecocriticism, cultural anthropology, political and social ecology and so on. Humans have been engaged in a meaningful intellectual dialogue with the earth as a category since the post-Second World War period, but the planet as a category was not visible earlier. Now, under the threat of global warming, humans have come face to face with planetary categories as well, aided by post-humanist scholars like Bruno Latour. This marks the beginning of a communicative relationship between humans and the planet. Now the way has been paved for the emergence of the planet as a historical category. The formalized emergence of planetary humanities as another useful conceptual category is just a matter of time. Historians need to connect deep and recorded histories and establish conversational links between the historical time and geological and biological times. This will enable the historians to tell the larger story of how a particular biological species, Homo sapiens, along with its Technosphere, as well as other species that co-evolved with or were dependent on them, came to dominate the entire planet within a short span of time.

The human–nature interface has been the most fundamental issues in whatever decisions human society has taken since time immemorial. One of the aspects of the inner conflicts within human societies of the past was fuelled by the continuous effort to resolve the question relating to the legitimate use of the natural world. As human settlements spread across the earth and as technology advanced, the urge to resolve this fundamental question intensified. An overarching denial of this issue by humankind, armed with the Technosphere, especially in recent decades, has completely disrupted the natural balance of the planet. It is now the final call for historians to address and resolve this fundamental question. The connection between the legitimate use of natural world and its connection with power and profit has put environmental issues on an equal footing with historical categories like race, class, gender, ethnicity, and nationalism. However, even in the face of a growing environmental crisis, humanity has shown a kind of indifference to environmental issues while giving more emphasis to power and politics. The present series, like many others in recent years, urge historians to reorient minds to the need of the hour, i.e. concern for Planet Earth.

The present series 'Reconnecting with the Nature' contains four different monographs: Rup Kumar Barman's *River, Society and Culture: Environmental Perspectives on the Rivers of Assam and Bengal*; Nupur Dasgupta's *Indian Medicinal Plants in the Shifting Terrains of Science: Botanical and Medical Literature of Nineteenth-century Bengal*; Anuradha Roy's *Rethinking Human–Animal Relationship: Reading Stories from Bengali Literature*; and Mahua Sarkar's *The Gasping City: An Environmental History of Calcutta, 1817–1923* is the outcome of a commendable effort towards re-establishing the human–nature interface.

River, Society and Culture: Environmental Perspectives on the Rivers of Assam and Bengal critically analyses the migration crisis and river–human relationships. The discourse offers an understanding of the lesser-explored society and culture of the Titash-Tista-Kalahi-Raidak basins of Bengal, Assam, and Bhutan from an environmental perspective. *Indian Medicinal Plants in the Shifting Terrains of Science: Botanical and Medical Literature of Nineteenth-century Bengal* traces the processes of medical and botanical reconnaissance during the nineteenth century, with a focus on indigenous medicinal plants, and also observes their integration into the framework of modern science. In *Rethinking Human–Animal Relationship: Reading Stories from Bengali Literature*, the author argues that animal studies should be considered a growing interdisciplinary field. The historiography of this field shows a 'moral schizophrenia' of human beings towards animal 'others'. It further seeks to connect the unrelenting exploitation of animals throughout history to the domination of humans by humans—oppression of women, racial and community struggles, etc. Finally, *The Gasping City: An Environmental History of Calcutta, 1817–1923* begins with an explanation of the intricate relationship between the development of cityscapes and its impact on the surrounding environment. Set between the period of 1817 and 1923, it also analyses the responses and attitudes of the educated urban people to ongoing environmental changes. Whether the traits of a 'planned city' was compatible or incompatible with the sustainable growth of environment is the main thrust area of this monograph.

With the publication of the present series—'Reconnecting with Nature'—I have no doubt that the immense potentials and possibilities of environmental history will be further refurbished. The grand quest to reach a resolution pertaining to the legitimate use of nature, I believe, will continue to dominate the discipline of history and its related knowledge systems. Environmental histories and environmental humanities will continue to thrive because the seeds of a new social and cultural history are firmly embedded in it. The importance of the present series has to be understood in this broader context.

RANJAN CHAKRABARTI

Note on the Series

Could history have been made without nature as the nurturing site for living species, without the primordial bounty of water, flora, and fauna? How did the hominids create their own space in this, the rarest of planets in the known orbit of the universe? How well have we been able to attain and preserve this? Can we sustain this with the progression of 'civilization' as we understand it? These are fundamental matters in environmental studies today and the questions take us beyond the rigidly defined contours of the discipline of history, which was specifically built around the human species. History is now observed to include much wider frames and perspectives.

The Department of History, Jadavpur University, is the first academic institution in the country to begin running a UGC-sponsored DRS Project on the History of Environment, with Professor Ranjan Chakravarti as the coordinator, from 2005. He successfully built the foundations of the discipline in the department. Within a decade, the programme achieved the level of a UGC DSA-I Special Assistance Project in 2015. The project has then been steered successively by Professor Amit Bhattacharya and Professor Mahua Sarkar. I was put in charge in 2018 and have supervised the programme till its completion in 2020. The department has witnessed a long tradition of research in the history of environment and allied subjects. The last few years from 2018 to 2020 saw a fresh bout of research by the faculty. The proposal for the publication of a few such research works was approved by the authorities of Jadavpur University in 2019–20. The outcome is showcased in the present series of books. The series consists of four short monographs, each devoted to a different theme, embodying distinct areas of research under the overarching theme of environmental history. The authors focus on elemental nature and human life around it. Thus, rivers, flora, fauna, and ecology in the urban context have been chosen as the major sites of investigation. The discussions here are distinctly designed to present new perspectives. An inkling of the overall philosophy of research has been briefly raised above. The authors, in their various contexts and approaches, project the deeper urge of the historian to illuminate the profundity of the existence of life on the Blue Planet. This short note to the series does not intend to delve any deeper into the themes and the underlying concerns they present. These have been discussed in detail in the authors' respective Introductions to their books.

I end this note by extending my thanks to those without whose support we could not have run the programme nor would this series have seen the light of day. First and foremost, I am beholden to the Hon'ble Vice-Chancellor of Jadavpur University, Professor Suranjan Das, for constant academic inspiration and advice. My sincerest thanks go to him and the authorities of the university for providing all the facilities required for carrying out the long-term project in the Department of History. I must express my deepest gratitude to all my colleagues in the department and outside it for their unstinted support. I am indebted to Professor Ranjan Chakrabarti, Professor Amit Bhattacharya, and Professor Mahua Sarkar, who were extremely generous in offering help and advice in running the programme and in carrying out the task of publications. Professor Anuradha Roy and Professor Rup Kumar Barman have been ready with all suggestions and help about the publication process. Sri Hemendranath Mandal, Sri Bholanath Mandal, and Sri Ritwik Bagchi, the research assistants associated with the programme, deserve high praise for helping me to carry out my duties throughout these years. The office staff, the librarians, and the library staff of the department have been extremely helpful and diligent in providing all support. I am ever so grateful for that. Finally, we owe much to our publishers, Primus Books, for ready support and for keeping us on schedule. I especially thank Mr B.N. Varma for showing interest in the project. Dr Prasun Chatterjee has extended great support through the process of publication, without which our project might have languished. I would like to extend profuse thanks to Ms Jyotika Mansata for taking the utmost care in preparing the manuscripts. Finally, I acknowledge with the deepest gratitude our indebtedness to the University Grants Commission for making it possible for the whole project and this series to come to fruition.

NUPUR DASGUPTA

Acknowledgements

Since the inception of the University Grants Commission-sponsored Special Assistance Programme (SAP) in 2005, the Department of History (Jadavpur University, Kolkata) has been engaged in exploring various aspects of environmental history. As a faculty member of the Department of History, I myself have undertaken a few pilot projects on several facets of environmental studies (including environment-induced migration, management of natural resources, crisis migration, nature-community relationship, folk medicinal practices and traditional technology).

This current monograph is based on the findings of three such pilot projects I completed between 2012 and 2020. I am indebted to the University Grants Commission for its generous assistance in my research on environmental history. I would like to express my sincere gratitude to Professor Suranjan Das, Honourable Vice-Chancellor of Jadavpur University. He has always been a source of inspiration for my research projects. I am also grateful to Professor Ranjan Chakraborty, Professor Amit Bhattacharya, Professor Mahua Sarkar and Professor Nupur Dasgupta, who have encouraged my studies on environmental history in different capacities.

RUP KUMAR BARMAN

Introduction

Since the beginning of settled human society, the rivers of South Asian countries have been intrinsically connected to societal evolution, especially in the context of the history of India and its neighbouring countries. From the Brahmaputra in the east to the Indus in the west and from the Ganga-Jamuna in the north to the Krishna-Kaveri in the south, these rivers and their innumerable tributaries have been accepted as the heart of Indian civilization and culture. However, geomorphological changes, climate change, construction of dams, barrages and power projects, dumping of garbage, gentrification, and indiscriminate exploitation of river systems have not only diminished the sacred nature of South Asian rivers but also contributed to the slow process of migration of people who lived in their basins.

Though social scientists have paid more attention to the conflict-induced, development-based and disaster-induced forced migration, as students of history we have noticed that the slow process of climate-induced migration of people from the river basin has been a common issue in the Indian subcontinent since the Indus Valley civilization. This is quite conspicuous in north-east India and Bangladesh. Heavy rainfall, adverse climatic conditions, soil structure and chain of rivers are closely connected with settlement patterns, traditional occupations and regional culture. However, migration of people has now become a perennial issue in West Bengal, Assam and Bangladesh because of geological forces and human intervention on the natural drainage systems. As this process works very slowly, it often remains beyond the attention of river studies. I have analysed this issue in the first chapter of this volume in the context of fisherman of Eastern Bengal and the Titash River. With the help of a Bengali novel by Adwaita Malla Barman, I have come to understand that the fishermen of eastern Bengal had a very close relationship with the source of their livelihood, i.e. the river. The traditional fishermen were forced to migrate from the river basin due to the rise in the silt bed. They lost their means of survival when the river system gradually dried up.

Rivers are also closely allied with political movements and the local population's struggle for survival. In the second chapter I have highlighted that the rivers of northern West Bengal and Assam as not only the nuclei of local culture and identity but also symbols of prosperity. Through the analysis of two novels, I discuss how the people of the Tista basin of North Bengal and the Kalahi basin of Assam have raised their voice against the disruptive impact of population growth, state policies and political changes.

The third chapter critically examines the cultural dimension of a transnational river called the Raidak, which flows from Bhutan to Bangladesh through

India. Here, I explore how the Raidak (called the Wang Chhu in Bhutan) symbolizes the national culture of Bhutan, and has led to the growth of a mixed culture in along the India–Bangladesh border.

1

Fishermen and Crisis Migration

An Environmental Study of *A River Called Titash*

And the Malos' right was in the flowing water, in its formless, groundless ever-moving fluidity. That right never found the solid touch of real ground, it never had a stable support, a hard foothold. Hence they are the floaters. No matter how much they, the fishermen, befriend the tree and the homes on the ground, they remain floating like vapour. No matter how hard they cling to the bosom of the earth, the soil of the earth is forever pushing them away: 'No space for you, no place for you!' As long as there is water in the river, only that long do they float on the water. When water dries, they too evaporate and disappear.

— Adwaita Malla Barman
A River Called Titash

Riverine Bengal is a prominent region of the Indian subcontinent known for its productive fishing sector. Numerous rivers, *beels*, *baors* (flood plain lakes) and tanks in Bengal are producers of a variety of fishes. Naturally, the fishermen and fish-consumers have a close relationship with the rivers and coastal belt.

However, state intervention, changes in management, technology and growth of pisciculture has changed the traditional relationship between the rivers and the fishermen.

On the other hand, ecological changes in the river system due to floods, soil erosion, rise of the silt bed and human intervention have created a huge number of environmental refugees. Thus, natural disasters and 'environmental degradation' have forced a 'crisis migration' of individuals and communities from Bengal (both Bangladesh and West Bengal), Assam and Tripura. This trend of forced migration in the recent years has been defined as 'environment-induced migration', 'climate change-induced forced migration', or 'crisis-induced forced migration'.[1] In the South Asian context, 'environment-induced crisis migration' is an alarming trend especially in the coastal belts and along riverbanks.

Bengal, the land of water, produces a great number of 'environment-induced forced migrants' every year. Along with empirical studies, Bengali literature can be helpful to conceptualize this trend. A literary illustration of 'crisis-induced forced migration' can be found in a well-known Bengali novel titled *A River Called Titash* by Adwaita Malla Barman (1914–51). Adwaita's account impresses upon readers the pathetic condition of the 'Malo fishermen' of eastern Bengal due to changes in the internal course of the Titash. This novel is extremely relevant in the context of environment-induced forced migration studies. In this chapter, I will analyse this novel in the context of environmental history and 'crisis-induced forced migration' from an environmental perspective.

The River System of Bengal and Bengali Novels

The river system of undivided Bengal can be divided into six groups according to their origin and course: Northern System, North-eastern System, Central Bengal System, South-eastern System, Western System and Tidal System of Southern Bengal. Rivers of the Northern System (mostly originating from Tibet, Sikkim, and Bhutan) flow downwards through the northern districts of West Bengal and Bangladesh. The Tista, the Baro Ranjeet, the Chhoto Ranjeet, the Balason, the Torsha, the Raidak, the Sankosh, the Karotoya, the Kaljani, the Mansai, the Jaldhaka, the Singimari, the Gadhadhar, the Mahananda, the Punarbhaba, the Kulik, the Nagar, the Gamiri, the Kalindi, the Girmati, the Pagla, the Baramasia, the Tangon, etc., are notable rivers in this system. The rivers of north Bengal are comparatively poorer in terms of availability of water throughout the year.

The North-eastern System, comprising the rivers of the Brahmaputra system and the Barak valley, mostly flow through the north-eastern districts of Bangladesh. Important rivers of this system include the Brahmaputra and its tributaries. The South-eastern System, on the other hand, originate mostly from the hill tracts of north-east India. The Karnafulli, the Pheni, the Sangu, the Matamuri, the Halda, the Chandkhali, the Titash, the Dakatia, the Bijay, the Ghumti, etc., are the major rivers of this system. This system covers the south-eastern part of Bangladesh.

The rivers of the Central Bengal System like the Ganges, the Bhagirathi or the Hooghly, the Padma, the Bhairav, the Jalangi, the Mathabhanga, the Churni, the Jamuna, the Kirtinasa, the Buri Ganga, the Dhaleswari, the Arial Khan, the Lakshya, the Madhumati, the Meghna, etc., and their tributaries have a comparatively higher availability of water. This system covers the districts of central Bengal including Murshidabad, Nadia, Dacca, Faridpur, Bakharganj, Jessore, etc.

The rivers of the Western System flow through the districts of Birbhum, Bankura, Bardhaman (Purba Bardhaman and Paschim Bardhaman), Medinipur (Purba Medinipur, Paschim Medinipur and Jhargram) and Purulia. Rivers in this region flow in a south-east direction from the west. Among the important rivers of the region, mention may be made of the Damodar, the Kana Damodar, the Mayurakshi, the Behula, the Dwarkeswar, the Ajay, the Kana Dwarkeswar, the Kumar, the Khari, the Banka, the Kangsabati, the Brahmani, the Kassai, the Silabati, the Rupnarayan, the Kelighai, the Rasulpur, the Subarnarekha, the Bakreswar, the Dwarka, the Pagla, the Banslai, etc. The rivers of this region are also less productive in terms of fish like the rivers of north Bengal.

However, the rivers in the extreme south of Bengal, including the tidal system, are rich in fish production throughout the year. Important rivers of this system are the Hooghly, the Kalindi, the Ichhamati, the Raimangal, the Bantala, the Saptamukhi, the Piyali, the Matla, the Bidhyadhari, the Thakuran, the Kaikalmari, the Haribhanga, the Garba, the Jamira, the Gosaba, the Haroagang, the Kultigang, the Kalgachia, etc.

Besides the rivers, there are a considerable number of tanks and canals in Bengal (constructed by the state and wealthy men) as well as *beels* (see Table 1.1) and *baors* (flood plain lakes) Besides the internal water bodies, Bengal includes a large coastal area extending from Chittagong to Medinipur through Khulna, Barishal and 24 Parganas districts.

TABLE 1.1: A List of Some Notable *Beels* of Colonial Bengal

Districts	*Notable Beels*
Rangpur	Barabeel, Churdda Bhuban, Nalagachi, Chikli, Kukrul and Hatia.
Mymensingh	Bagjan, Rakdaha, Karatia, Phatikjani, Nadial, Baigunbari, etc.
Bagura	Balighata, Satulgari, Chirla, Kastagari, Chubri, Ratnapur Beel, Iswardhari Beel, Chalan Beel, etc.
Pabna	Bara Beel, Sonapati, Ghugudaha Beel, etc.
Maldah	Bamanghata Beel, Jagaddal Beel, Raniganj Beel, Bhaiyar Beel, Saolmari Beel, Dagun Beel, Kowa Khen Beel, Sabdalpur Beel, Mirzapur Beel, Karun Khali Beel, Sukur Bari, Baragharia Beel, Haripur, Kammar, Sarjan Mallikpur, Chana, Parsan Beel, Dhajora, Madaripur, Gandaill, Bhattia Beel, etc.
Murshidabad	Bhandardah, Soula Beel, Muti Jhil, etc.
Noakhali	Dhagaria, Parkot, Alipur, Kashimnagar, Badarpur, Hasamandi, etc.
Tippera	Atkapa, Alta, Bahjani, Bara Beel, Bandgarh Beel, Baralla Beel, Chantar Beel, Kajla Beel, Kakai, Khola, Mondahare, etc.

Districts	*Notable Beels*
Bakharganj	Adampura, Ashkar, Baghia, Battaridaua, Baldia, Bama, Dapura, Daumara, Dharindia, Harta, Jhanjharia, Kalareja, Ramsil, Rampur Chiharia, Salti, Suja, etc.

Source: Author.

A close relationship exists between the rivers and coastal belts and their local populations. Such water bodies are the source of livelihood for traditional fishermen. This nature-community relationship has been an important source of inspiration for Bengali novelists, starting from Bankim Chandra Chattopadhyay (1838–94) to Harisankar Jaladas (1953–present). These writers examine the role of rivers in the socio-economic life of Bengal. There are large variations in the Bengali novels that deal with rivers and their people (particularly fishing communities). The first category of novels comprises those that are not directly related to fishermen; instead, they focus on the lives of the non-fishing communities in the region. The novels in the second category portray romanticized versions of the lives of fishermen. The novels in the third category are more authentic as sources for the contemporary socio-political and cultural history of fishing communities. These are written by novelists who have direct knowledge of fishing and fishery management.

Bankim Chandra Chattopadhyay, the pioneer Bengali novelist, left an impression of the marginalized social status of the fisherwomen of Bengal (although he never attempted to write about the fishermen) in his work *Devi Chaudhurani* (1882). His *Kopal Kundala* (1866), *Bishabrikshya* (1873) and *Chandra Sekhar* (1975) also mention the river systems of Bengal.

Rabindranath Tagore (1861–1941) was fascinated with the Padma River. His *Galpaguchha* depicts the rural lives of the people living along the Padma. His short stories, such as 'Post Master', 'Shasti', 'Durbuddhi', 'Megh O Roudra', and 'Khokababur Prattabattan', etc., demonstrate the effect the Padma had on his mind. *Gora* (1920) is an exceptional novel, where he highlights the conflict between the local peasants and the State, while another novel, *Naukadubi* (1906), focuses on the river systems and water transport of Bengal.

River systems are also an important theme in the works of Sharat Chandra Chattopadhyaya (1876–1938). His *Shrikanta* (1917) vividly describes the rivers of Bengal. Tarasankar Bandyopadhyaya's (1898–1971) novels *Chaitali Ghurni*, *Gana Debata*, *Kalindi*, and *Hasuli Baker Upakatha* also occasionally impress the importance of rivers in village society upon their readers.

The novels of Saroj Kumar Ray Choudhury—*Mayurakshi*, *Grihakopoti*, and *Somlata*—are set against the background of rural Bengal. Buddhadev Guha, another notable novelist, in his *Koyeler Kachhe*, also highlights the lives of the village people in the basin of the Koyel River in Hazaribag-Giridi.

The river system of northern Bengal has gained attention from Bengali novelists in recent times. *Lalmati* (1951) and *Mahananda* (1951) by Narayan Gangopadhyaya (1918–70), *Madhu Sadhu Khan* (1988) by Amiya Bhusan Majumdar (1918–2001) and *Uttaradhikar* (1980) by Samaresh Majumdar (1982) have tangentially touched the role of the rivers, specifically the Mahananda and Tista, in the sociopolitical life of north Bengal. Debesh Ray is another notable contemporary novelist, whose work *Tista Parer Brittanta* (1988) is perhaps the most significant contribution to the literary world as it features descriptions of marginalized and indigenous people of postcolonial South Asian countries, specifically north Bengal. Here, the Tista River is symbolic of the cultural lives of local communities.

There are a few other Bengali novels written about rivers and their local populations: *Padma* (1342) and *Kopabati* (1941) by Pramatha Nath Bishi, *Padma Pramatta Nadi* (1346) by Subodh Basu, *Icchamati* (1356 BS) by Bibhuti Bhushan Bandyopadhyaya (1894–1950), *Antarjali Jatra* (1369 BS) by Kamal Kumar Majumder (1914–79), *Jalangi* (1974) by Shoukat Osman (1917–98), *Jal Jangal* (1358 BS) by Manoj Basu, to name a few. Although these novels highlight different aspects of village communities living in the river basins, conceptualize processes of social change, and raise certain fundamental questions, the lives of the traditional fishermen are not at their core.

The first Bengali novel about fishermen and boatmen was *Padma Nadir Majhi* by Manik Bandyapadhyaya (1908–56). The protagonist of the novel, Kuber, and his fellow fishermen were completely dependent on the availability of fish in the Padma. However, the ordinary fishermen did not control fishing activities; in fact, they did not even own their own boats and nets. They worked as 'water labourers' on the boats of the middlemen/traders/moneylenders. On the other hand, some fishermen owned their boats and nets, allowing them a comparatively better economic status than the 'water labourers'. Dhananjay and Jagat are two characters in this novel who represent the second category of fishermen. But fishermen as a community were dependent on the whims of nature. In the novel, they lose everything, including their boats and nets, after a natural disaster takes place. They are forced to take loans from the moneylenders, transforming them into 'bonded people'. They are never released from their debt, and are forced to pay exorbitant rates of interest to the moneylenders. *Padma Nadir Majhi* thus provides an impactful, realistic image of the traditional fishermen and boatmen of Eastern Bengal.

Ganga by Samaresh Basu is another novel based on the lives of the fishermen dependent on 'capture fishing' in big rivers and in the sea. The main character of this novel is Bilas, who hails from the particular fishing caste (like Malo); however, all traditional fishermen castes of Bengal (including Kaibartya, Poundra, Rajbanshi, Nikari, Chunari, etc.,) have been equally represented in this novel. The traditional fishermen of 24 Parganas (north and south), their modes of fishing and marketing, and their exploitation by the *mahajans* (moneylenders) have been critically examined by Basu. *Char Kasem* (1356) by Amarendra Ghosh is another novel about the fishermen of the Padma, which reflects their struggles in the silt bed of the river. *Ilish Marir Char* (1368) by Abdul Jabbar and *Padmar Palidvip* (1986) by Abu Ishak are also based on the lives of traditional fishermen.

In the twenty-first century, a few Bengali novels on rivers and coastal have drawn much attention from readers. Among them, Harisankar Jaladas's novel *Jalaputra* (2008) is unique. He categorically analyses the lives of the marine fishers of Chittagong, depicting the internal contradictions within the community as well as the impact of both natural disasters and capitalistic intervention in marine fishing.

However, among Bengali novels, our focus in this chapter is on *Titash Ekti Nadir Naam* (*A River Called Titash*) by Adwaita Malla Barman. Long before the adoption of international covenants, conventions and guidelines for 'environment-included displaced persons' (2001) Adwaita highlighted such 'crisis-induced migration' from a literary perspective.

The Malo Fishermen of Colonial Bengal

The protagonists of *A River Called Titash* belong to the Malo community (or Jhalo Malo) whose lives are dependent on fishing. Being a Malo, Adwaita was not dependent on literary imagination to portray the life and culture of the community. His personal experience as a Malo of Gokarnaghat village on the bank of the Titash in eastern Bengal (Brahmanbaria, Comilla) contributed to him gaining a permanent place of honour in the literary world. Before analysing *A River Called Titash*, through the lens of environmental history, let us first discuss the historical context of the Malos of colonial Bengal.

Malos or Jhalo Malos are traditional fishermen of eastern and north-eastern India, particularly Bengal, Assam, Meghalaya, and Tripura. They have been living in these regions since the very beginning of settled human civilization.[2] Though precolonial Bengali and

Kamrupi literatures reference this community, we cannot estimate their population distribution and mode of life before the beginning of the colonial period. Among the colonial administrators who carried-out systematic surveys of the caste and tribal communities of eastern India, Buchanan Hamilton was the first to study the Malos. During his survey (1807–14) of Assam, Bengal, Bihar and Uttar Pradesh, Buchanan described the social, economic and cultural lives of the Malos of Calcutta, Dinajpur, Goalpara, Rangpur and Maimensingh.[3] Regarding the Jhalo Malos of Rangpur and Goalpara, he said: 'The Jhalo, fishermen of the Kaiborta Caste not above hundred houses; Malo, another caste of fishermen, contains a great number of people, especially on the banks of the river above Calcutta. They are fishermen, and do not use anything, which the Brahmins consider grossly impure.'[4] Buchanan had estimated the settlement of around one thousand fishermen families in Goalpara. Regarding Dinajpur, he highlighted that 'fishermen in general are not so poor as the common labour, who are employed in agriculture, the whole number in the district may be about 2,500 houses'.[5] Buchanan also gave a detailed account of the nets, boats, fishing and fish processing methods of the Malos of Dinajpur, Rangpur and Goalpara. But the Malos of other districts did not draw his attention, because of which we cannot estimate the population of the entire Malo community of the early nineteenth century.

However, with the establishment of the census in India in 1872, the Malos received considerable attention from the colonial government. We can get an idea about the distribution of the Jhalo Malos in the late nineteenth century from this census data, as seen in Table 1.2. This table shows that the Malos were concentrated in Mymensingh, Comilla, Dacca, Pabna, Jessore, Khulna, Nadia, Murshidabad, Hooghly, Rangpur, Rajshahi, 24 Parganas, Faridpur and Bakharganj districts which are teeming with of rivers, *beels* and *baors*. However, due to the partition of the state in 1947, the Malos of eastern Bengal, along with other minority communities, migrated en masse to Assam, Tripura, West Bengal, Uttar Pradesh, Orissa, Bihar and other provinces of India. According to the census of 2001, the total population of the Jhalo Malos in West Bengal is only 2,93,714. In Assam and Meghalaya they were 77,533 and 1,469 Jhalo Malos, respectively, in 2001. In Tripura, the Malos are considered Kaibartyas and are, hence, difficult to distinguish from the latter population. At the same time, the Malos also have a considerable presence in Bangladesh. Thus, it is difficult to estimate the exact present-day figures for Malos in India and Bangladesh.

TABLE 1.2: Distribution of the Jhalo/Jelia and Malos of Bengal (1872 and 1881)

District	*1872 (Jhalo/Jelia)*	*1872 (Malo)*	*1881 (Jhalo/Jelia)*	*1881 (Malo)*
Bardhaman	10,533	9,333	5,374	454
Bankura	1,261	6,933	3,310	22,079
Birbhum	765	586	4,059	3,158
Medinipur	29,450	39,804	20,063	40,236
Hooghly	15,829	1,820	10,369	2,097

District	*1872 (Jhalo/Jelia)*	*1872 (Malo)*	*1881 (Jhalo/Jelia)*	*1881 (Malo)*
Howrah	15,829	1,820	10,369	2,097
24 Parganas	23,979	2,333	11,424	1,542
Nadia	20,398	13,311	14,998	10,672
Khulna	—	—	20,925	3,390
Jessore	43,642	12,600	36,836	10,765
Murshidabad	3,014	7,386	2,848	7,598
Dinajpur	10,296	1,203	13,398	1,222
Rajshahi	16,692	1,768	13,774	1,484
Rangpur	16,301	1,392	8,387	1,148
Bogra	5,162	3,637	5,218	1,120
Pabna	26,945	16,490	39,260	6,566
Darjeeling	44	26	13	1,175
Jalpaiguri	1,370	251	3,870	3
Kuch Behar	—	—	2,640	133
Dacca	32,269	6,437	40,733	1,949
Faridpur	20,460	6,033	28,607	2,389
Bakerganj	12,602	1,751	13,183	989
Mymensingh	36,399	13,999	34,887	11,454
Tipperah	7,105	2,600	12,516	1,720
Chittagong	9,284	525	15,312	31
Noakhali	9,828	110	8,602	—
Hill Tracts	—	—	11	—

Source: Rup Kumar Barman, Final Report of ICSSR Sponsored Project titled *Changing Nature of Caste*, Kolkata: Jadavpur University, 2017.

The colonial administrators and census enumerators also stated their opinions about the racial, physical and social status of the Jhalo Malos. Dr James Wise, a notable ethnographer of Dacca, wrote in 1883: 'They [Malos] are remarkable for strength, nerve, and independent bearing. The finest examples of Bengali manhood are found among them, and their muscular figures astonish those inhabitants of towns.'[6] This implies that the Jhalo Malos were not like ordinary Bengalis. According to Wise, the Malos had been living in the Bengal Delta since time immemorial. H.H. Risley (one of the most prominent administrative scholar-cum ethnographers of the colonial period) opined in 1891 that 'they are the remnants of a district aboriginal tribe, and not merely an occupational group'.[7] Colonial observations thus gave us the idea that the Malos were indigenous people of Bengal. Their indigenous features were also noted in such works, as well as their occupational behaviour, particularly their 'collective action' in fishing.

The Malos developed their own fishing methods as well as unique technique and technologies for making boats, nets, and fishing implements. As their livelihood was rooted in catching fish with different varieties of nets (such as *chhanda*, *utor*, *jhanki*, *sangla*, *gulti*, etc.), the Malos were entirely dependent on fish and rivers.[8] Members of the community also took up other professions such as agriculture and boating when fish were not available during some months. The colonial observers also recorded these non-fishing occupations followed by the Malos. Thus, Risley stated: 'Under the Muhammedan Government they served as boatmen, *chaprasis*, mace-bearer (*asabardar*), and staff bearer (*sonte-bordor*) in profession. They were also employed in conveying treasure from Dacca to Murshidabad.'[9] However, the Malos were, in essence, considered a fishing community.

The Malos were mainly internal captured fishers. This meant they were dependent on the internal water sources such as rivers, *beels* and *boors*. They had to pay taxes to zamindars who possessed the rights to fish in small water bodies and flood plain lakes. In most cases, the Malos would collectively lease the right to fish through their leader (*matabbar*). This trend of collective action contributed to the sustenance of their self (community) identity.

Economically, all Malos are not marginalized as wide class differences in the community have always existed. Those who had their own boats and nets were considered part of the first category. They used to employ other 'asset-less' Malos as co-fishers or as 'water-labourers'. As owners of the means of production, this class enjoyed considerable profits from their fishing operations. The *aratdars* and *nikaris* (commission agents) are also placed in the first category of fishermen. The fishermen of the second category were those who had their own boats and nets but did not employ any other Malos as co-fishers, but were aided by family members in their endeavours. They were thus independent fishermen but not marginalized.

However, the majority Malos fall into the third, and lowest, category. Individuals without boats, nets or other fishing implements were included in this class. They were basically 'share-fishers' or 'water-labourers' working under fishermen of the first category. The ordinary fish *paikars* (fish retailers) were also very poor like the fishermen of the third category. Like the latter, they too did not own any means of production, except for a pair of scales, a chopper, and earthen fish pots.

As fishermen, however, the Malos had a very strong 'community feeling' and 'community consciousness'. Although the fish they caught was in great demand among upper-caste Bengalis, the Malos as 'social beings' were considered inferior (*adham*, despicable creatures, or practically Untouchables) in society. This is clear evidence of the social disparity present in precolonial/colonial Bengali Hindu society. Thus, in spite of their internal class hierarchy, the Malos had a sense of communal unity; the concept of class was secondary to them. Their inferior social identity was the primary parameter of their existence in colonial society. Thus, despite Europeans touting Malos as the 'finest examples of Bengali manhood', educated caste-Hindus (including the prominent literary figures of Bengal) considered them to be at the bottom of the social hierarchy.[10]

The inferior social status of the Malos was also recorded in the administrative records of the colonial government. In 1891, Risley wrote:

> Malos, as a rule belong to the Vaishnava sect. Their Purohit is a Patit-Brahman, and their Guru is a Gossain.... The dead are usually burned on the bank of a river, and the ashes cast into the water. *Sraddh* is performed on the thirty first day after death.... The social rank of the Malos is low, and Brahmans will not take water from their hands. The only titles met with among Malos are Majhi, Patra, and Bepari.[11]

This comment indicates the nature of 'social injustices' faced by the Malos. Uneducated members of the community (with no knowledge of the traditional Hindu scriptures) could not raise questions against such scriptural dictums. However, at the turn of the twentieth century, a section of Malos began to empower themselves through modern education. The Malos who entered the educational institutes established by the colonial government and Christian missionaries, gained considerable knowledge about colonial laws and courts, the judiciary, rule of law and, of course, about 'rationalism' (which formed the main parameters of modernism).[12] Modern education hence motivated them to protest against the 'social injustices' they faced in order to gain 'social respect'.

The only available alternative for the Malos to gain 'respect' in the caste-oriented colonial society was to take the initiative to construct a respectable identity. Like other lower caste communities (Rajbanshis, Poundras, Namasudras, Bhuinmalis, Sunris, Dhobas, etc.), the educated Malos had developed a sense of 'self-respect' in the early twentieth century. Brajanath Das, Ananta Chandra Das Barman, Udvab Chandra Malla Barman, Shashi Bhushan Das Roy, Dinanath Talukdar, Suresh Chandra Barman, Prasanna Kumar Choudhury, and a few other notable Malos of Dacca, Mymensingh, Pabna, Bagura, Tripura, Jessore, Sylhet, and eastern Bengal founded the Jhalla Malla Kshatriya Samity in 1913. This organization was passionate about establishing the Malos as a respectable kshatriya community of Bengal; they believed this would make up for the social injustices they had faced previously. Mahendra Nath Malla Barman and Dharma Chand

Malla Barman, two notable Malo experts on Sanskrit literature, argued in their writings that the Jhalo Malos were basically the offspring of the kshatriyas of the Jhalwar and Malla kingdoms of Rajasthan. These groups had migrated to Bengal from western India due to regional political crises. According to Mahendra Nath:

> The Jhalo Malos are no way the people of mixed or inferior sub-caste. Manu had described them as 'Bratya Kshatriyas'. We do also consider the Jhalo-Malos as Bratya Kshatriyas. Since they did not follow the rituals of *upanayan* for holding *paita* (sacred threat), they are Bratya Kshatriyas. The Kshatriya migrants from Malabar and Jhalarkot and their offspring have been identified as Jhalos and Malos in Bengal according to the names of the land of their ancestors. So the Jhalos and Malos are not different caste, but the two names of same community.[13]

Mahendra Nath also argued in 1914 that fishing was not an inferior occupation in ancient India; hence, fishermen were not Untouchables and were well-respected in ancient society. The marriage between the King Santanu and the fishergirl Satyabati (of the *Mahabharata*) exemplified the respectable status of the fishermen in the ancient period. Mahendra Nath also raised the point that in the *Mahabharata* 'a golden fish was fixed as a target for Arjun for establishing marriage relation with Draupadi'. Therefore, fishing as a profession could not destroy the caste status of a community. He wrote:

> Being born from the womb of the fisher girl (*Matsyagandha*), Byasdev is revered in the entire Hindu society. He is immortal in the world because of compiling *Puranas*,

history and composing *Bhagwat* of the Hindu society. If he had had been considered inferior, being born from a fisher mother, the leaders of the Hindus would not have shown their respect to the feet of Byasdev.... 'profession can't destroy the caste of any community'. And fish is always consumable. Hence fish is killable. We do notice even today the Brahmins as sellers of fish being the owners of hotel. The Kayasthays are selling processed fish and meat in their hotels. Soon after getting down from trains, boats and ships we listen to the call of the Brahmin hotel-owners that 'come to my hotel where fish and *dal* (pulses) are available'. Are these people not sellers of fish?[14]

In spite of constructing an imaginary kshatriya identity (at least in literary works), the Malos were not recognized as Kshatriyas in the early twentieth century. Therefore, they approached the colonial government to record themselves as 'Malla Kshatriyas'. At the same time, the Malos gave considerable attention to the spread of education among members of their community. An analysis of the contents of *Jhal Mal Bandhav* (a Malo journal) shows that the Malos had considerable presence in white-collar jobs—government offices, schools, colleges, medical practices and the engineering sector—in the 1920s and 1930s, particularly in Bengal, Bihar, Assam and Burma. The educated Malos rejected the custom of observing *shradha* ceremony thirty days after the death of an individual. Like the caste kshatriyas, they reduced this mourning period to thirteen days. At the same time, they begun to adopt caste kshatriya surnames like Malla Barman, Jhalla Barman, Singha Barman, and Das Barman and discarded traditional family names (Malo, Jhalo, Byepari and Patra).

Adwaita Malla Barman was born into a fishing community on 1 January 1914 in Gokarnaghat village of Brahmanbaria, Tipperah (Comilla) district. His father, Adhar Chandra, was a fisherman of the third category. In his early life, Adwaita lost his parents and siblings due to abject poverty. At that time, The 'Malla kshatriya movement' had a great impact in Gokarnaghat due to which Adwaita was admitted to school by his uncle, Shri Sanatan Malla Barman. He completed his matriculation from Edward Institution of Brahmanbaria and took admission in Victoria College in Comilla. However, his financial condition prevented Adwaita from continuing his studies for long. He left for Calcutta in 1934 in search of a job and worked as a journalist at numerous publication such as *Tripura*, *Nabashakti*, *Dainik Ajad*, *Nabajug*, *Krishak*, *Jugantar*, *Desh* and *Ananda Bazar Patrika*. Here, Adwaita cultivated his literary skills. In Calcutta, he produced his best writings including three novels, five short stories, a few poems, one translation and twenty-five essays. Among these works, *A River Called Titash* is considered to be most significant. It was originally published in the *Mohammadi* in serialized form in the late 1940s and then published as a novel in 1956 after Adwaita had passed away.

Malo Society and Economy in *A River Called Titash*

Malo society as described in *A River Called Titash* is very similar to what I have discussed in the previous section of this chapter. Adwaita classified the Malos into four categories: (i) big fishermen, (ii) independent fishermen, (iii) marginal fishermen, and (iv) fishermen-cum-agriculturists. The 'big fishermen' of the novel were those who owned nets, boats and other capitalistic means for fishing. They used to hire marginalized fishermen as labourers and had every opportunity of surplus appropriation. Banshiram Mondol, Kalobaran Byapari and Bodhai Malo were such fishermen in the novel. According to Adwaita:

> Bodhai Malo of Nayanpur village is much bigger in money [*sic*] than all the other Malos there. His house has four or five rooms roofed with corrugated tin. He has two sons making money. He is big and dark like an elephant, and strong too. His fishing and dealing in fish is of a different kind. He leases large ponds and tanks, and stocks them with fry. Later on, with the help of his two sons and some hired hands, he hauls up batches of grown fish and supplies distant markets. Sometimes he hires many hands in this business. When the rivers dry and the Malos see nothing but darkness before their eyes, they go to Bodhai's house hoping to be hired.[15]

The big fishermen had maximum share in the profit generated through fishing operation and business. The hired Malos were compelled to accept minimum share (or wage) as fixed by them.

There are also examples of independent Malos in the novel. These Malos owned their own boats and nets but did not hire any Malo labourers. However, they would share their boats and nets with co-fishers. The best example of this kind of fishermen as described in *A River Called Titash* is Kishore. In the novel, Gagan Malo and his son 'Subal' were such fishermen. According to the novelist:

> Subal's father Gagan Malo never owned a boat and net. All his life he was hauling fish in others' boats with other's nets.... Thus when Subal's father dies, he is unable to leave his son with a boat and net of his own. When Subal grows up to a man's height, he joins Kishore in his boat and keeps on casting nets with Kishore.[16]

In his novel, Adwaita described a fourth, and different, category of Malos in eastern Bengal, i.e. fishermen-cum-agriculturists. Adwaita's states:

> Another marvellous thing Kishore has noticed. The homes in this village (Sukdevpur) have not only nets but also ploughs, the tools for fishing on one side and the tools for tilling on the other! Almost every home has the vat of resin (*gaab*), the bundles of net, the fishing ropes and baskets as prominently visible as the plough and yoke, the weeder and the ladder.[17]

The Malos of this category were less likely to participate in crisis-induced migration as they would not be ruined by changes in the course of the river.

In spite of economic 'differences', the Malos as a caste community were strongly united. Adwaita's novel shows that the concept of *samaj* (a social unit or group), and the tradition of 'collective action' in economic bargaining (leasing water bodies or fixing of rents) and resolving social disputes strengthened social bonds among the Malos. At the same time, despite their best efforts to represent themselves as ksatriyas, Malos were considered inferior by their upper-caste neighbours. Even in the face of such oppression, the Malos were identified as a 'social community' for whom 'economic difference' or 'class' as a parameter of stratification did not apply. According to Adwaita:

A Malo's first duty is to maintain unity in the community, to care for the feelings and interests of other Malos in the neighbourhood, because they have only each other. Those other communities ... don't let any Malo in their homes. Anything touched by a Malo is considered polluted. At their festivals and at worship, even the Malos, who are invited must themselves dispose of the banana leaves they eat from, because their high-caste status will be polluted if they touch them.[18]

Adwaita also raised a question regarding their low-caste status:

They [the upper castes] hold the Malos in such contempt: the Malos don't know how to read and write like them; how to walk like them dressed in dhoti and wrapper and shoes. But is that supposed to make them unworthy of even being touched by them? Are the Malos not human beings merely because they are Malos?[19]

The social injustice and humiliation faced by the Malos was described in great detail by Adwaita. He expressed his feelings as a Malo through a conversation between Dayalchand and Tamsir Baap, two minor characters in the novel:

Dayalchand goes on, skipping nothing, your [Tamshir Baap] hut is near the market place. We hear that the Kayasthas come to your home to practice tabla-playing and eye your daughters. Think of this, your mixing with the Kayasthas will not confer on you the rank of a Kayastha. You will always remain only a Malo. Even if you seat them on thrones when they visit you, they'll give you a broken old plank to sit on when you visit them. Even if you serve them tobacco in a silver *hookah*, they'll hand you a detached clay top, not the *hookah* they themselves use.[20]

Hence, it appears that the socio-economic condition of the Malos, as described by Adwaita, is not different from the image constructed by colonial observers. In fact, the novel contributes towards the construction of a historical pictures of the Malos and their lives.

Crisis, Displacement and Migration

It has been indicated earlier that economic crises or degradation in lifestyle often generates forces of migration. As a poet, novelist, columnist and essayist, Adwaita considered such crises to be very serious matters. In his schooldays, Adwaita illustrated the pathetic condition of the ordinary people of eastern Bengal and Tripura in a poem title 'Tripura Lakshmi' (composed in 1935).[21] Thus, it appears that Adwaita was concerned about starvation and scarcity of livelihood of the marginalized people of Bengal from a very early age.

Adwaita provided a picture of the crisis-ridden people of Bengal in his short story 'Death of Ashalata' (1948).[22] In this tale, he described the death of three women: the first, Ashalata Chakladar, died of starvation caused by a famine in the 1940s; the second, Ashalata Talukdar committed suicide in 1947 after she failed to maintain her modesty (due to a lack of clothes as her family lost all their belongings after the Partition of Bengal); the third, Ashalata Mondal, also committed suicide because of the mental trauma she faced after migrating from her homeland of East Bengal after Partition. This story depicts the three basic forces of forced migration: natural disaster, economic crisis and conflict.

Poverty and crisis-induced-migration were further explored by Adwaita in his essay-cum-open letter written in the context of Pearl S. Buck (1892–1973) receiving the Nobel Prize for the novel *The Good Earth* [23] Adwaita wrote to Buck in the context of 1940s Bengal:

> We have to cross the crowd of uncountable number of starved people in roads. They are the blueprints of the picture of people as illustrated by you. They have migrated to urban centres, being starved. A number of them have perished in their way while most of them reached to the city. Their women do not have clothes for keeping modesty. These women pick up the seeds of mangos left by the tired home-bound officials (*babus*) and feed them to their hungry children. Price of mango has increased. Its seed is not available. They search for food (with a mind of searching gold) as mixed with the rotten flesh of dog, cat and rat at the dustbin. Servants of westernized gentlemen's home scatter the rotted parts of breads to the clay heap beside the dustbin. They fight for that bread. They start crying if failed to catch it. Afterwards they die with an ironical laugh at the footpath. It is again more woeful matter that we do not have minimum civic arrangement to remove their dead bodies in proper time.[24]

This short paragraph aptly portrays the miserable condition of the ordinary population of Bengal during the Second World War. However, Adwaita left his best writing on the condition of nature-induced and crisis-induced forced migrants in *A River Called Titash*. This novel focuses on the Malo (or Jhalo Malo) fishing community who lives along the banks of the Titash and the Meghna in eastern Bengal.

At the beginning of this novel, Adwaita indicates the possibility of crises occurring in the lives of those Malos those who were completely dependent on 'internal captured fishing'. He describes that these Malos do not consider any other profession except fishing.

> Who are those people who live beside Titash? They are Malo men and women. All the paths from the yards of Malo homes lead to the water of Titash.... The Malo neighbourhoods are on the banks of the river Titash. The boats tied by the slope, the nets spread on the ground, the clay vat of *gaab* resin in a corner of each yard, in every home a set of distaff spindles and reels to spin thread and weave nets. With all these the Malos live their daily life.[25]
>
> ... The season of fishing is exhausted near the end of winter. Titash becomes tired from yielding to the Malos' unquenchable daily demand.... After spending an entire morning laying in and gathering up the net without getting a single fish, Kishore abruptly pulls in the net handle and says, 'Subla, let's go to the lake of Jagatpur. Just can't get the net and the fish together here.'
>
> But even after ruffling and churning the lake's bottomless waters with the poles of the net, they find no fish.... Kishore says, 'Want us to save ourselves, Subla? Then let's head north.'[26]

The mention of going 'north' indicates the migration of Malo fishermen to a new place in search of livelihood. However, this 'was a seasonal (temporary) migration', what the Malos refer to as '*khalabaoya*'. Adwaita mentions that the Malos on the Bijay riverbank tended to migrate temporarily in the dry season. According to the novel:

As the water drops to the bottom, the fish gasp for breath, holding their mouths out for air. The fisher folk too, like the fish, are left gasping. A time comes when they despair at the sight of the shadow of the dry skeleton of Mahakaal, the Time Eternal. Those who went away in the wet season on fishing trips to the big river of Chandpur now leave their boats and nets in charge of the 'commission agents' (*nikaris*), and take the train back home. They are the only ones who do not have to worry; they pass the hard time spending the cash they have brought. But those who did not leave the attachment of home while the river held enough water suffer the most hardship.[27]

The fisherfolk on the banks of the Titash would migrate to the fish-processing field (*khala*) at Ujaninagar (owned by Banshiram Mondol of Sukdevpur).

The chief (Banshiram Mondol) owns four large tanks. During monsoon, when the river overflows the banks, shoals of fish, many from great distances, swim into the tanks and congregate there. When the water starts receding, the chief's men come and dam those tanks, locking in thousands of large fish such as *rui*, *katla*, *nandil*, *mrigel*. In the dry season of winter and spring, Malo men and women from many communities of many different villages come together in one spot in this way. Large shacks are raised to last for six months, each shack the length of a full sprint in which they stay for the duration of the work.

People who have never seen each other gather here and become one huge family. They eat together, stay together and work together. Heaps of rise and huge quantity of vegetables are cooked in the way it is done for mass-feeding at big festivities. They sit down in long rows to eat. After eating and washing their hands and mouths in the river, they return to their work.

And what is the work they do all day? The women are sitting on the ground in long rows, each with the flat base of her fish cutter held between her toes. One group of men is bringing basketful of freshly hauled fish and unloading in piles before the women. The women's hands are working with the smooth swiftness of machines. In three moves, in a blink of their eyes, a large fish is gutted, cleaned and precisely thrown over their shoulders at the back, forming other piles, where another group of men is carrying the fish in basketfuls to the raised ground prepare for drying them. Day after day these works go on for three months. When the dried fish is sold off to merchants, they prepare to end their six-month trip away from their home regions and head back. They call it 'plying the fish-drying stretch.[28]

Thus, it seems that seasonal migration in search of livelihood was a common feature among the Malos, particularly those who did not have an alternative mode of earning a living. Those Malos who did agricultural work along with fishing were not compelled to migrate from their villages. According to Adwaita:

If some invisible saitan someday unties the knots of their nets, loosens the nails that hold their boats together, and if it drinks up the river's water in a giant draft, it will not be able to destroy them, because they can survive on the harvest of their land. Alongside doing the work of raising crops on the fields, their hand will be able to repair their nets and boats, return them to the way they were before, and await the rains to replenish the river. These Malos will never be ruined![29]

What would be future of the landless Malos if all the rivers dried up? The possibility of such a crisis was raised by Adwaita in the novel. He wrote that the life of peasants on the riverbanks was in no way secure.

The bosom of Bengal is draped with rivers and their tributaries, twisted and tangled like matted locks, specked with white of foamy waves. The verdant Bengal is like a maiden in the embrace of an ancient sage, held to his immense chest, locked in his wet kiss, his matted hair and beard tumbling in sinuous complexity over her youthful body and flowing down below. All those tangled, wet, gray locks are the rivers.

But all the rivers are not similar in appearance and essence. How they behave with people differs and how people behave with them differs; people who live beside them and use them and the people who live away from them but who also use them. All the rivers meet a great many needs of people's daily lives, but they do so in unique ways. The big ones are visited by merchant vessels with billowing sails. Fishermen's boats ply their huge expanses through the day, for a day at a time. The men cook and eat and sleep in their boats, and catch fish. In everything about those rivers is revealed a beauty that possesses a harsh form there. The bare banks of newly formed sand bars are lined with rows of coconut and areca nut palms. The sharp-edged currents undercut lands along the banks. The hard-hitting waves make huge chunks of the banks collapse and fall in. People's home, farmlands, granaries and rows of areca palm all helplessly tip over, break up, and drown! Nothing is spared, nothing is shown mercy. The river there is a frenzied sculptor at work, destroying and creating restlessly in crazed joy, riding the high-flying swing of fearsome energy ... that is one kind of art.[30]

However, the crisis that emerged in the lives of the Malos along the Titash riverbank was not related to soil erosion but to the rise of silt bed. Adwaita wrote:

One day, the floating silt bed is caught in the role of Mohon's net. It was the last day of an ebb tide: the big river has drawn away much and reduced Titash's water level, as it always does near the end of all ebbings, before returning it all with the high tide. During the ebb, even after giving much away, Titash still stays solemn with a deep body of water. The abundance in its midstream is never diminished.

Mohan's heart pounds like a hammer ... And this is in broad daylight, right before his human eyes. As soon as he lowers the net, its bamboo pole, even in midstream, hits ground at the bottom. The boat shudders, and so does Mohan.

After coming home, he remains in stunned silence. When the neighborhood folks call him for something, he explodes: 'Let the Malos do *jatra*, verse-singing, let them dance, let them fight and squabble, whatever they want. No need to worry for the future anymore. The river's dried.'

'What are you saying, Mohan? What did you just say, O Manmohan!'

'You heard what I said. Go in the river and check for yourself.'

Half a mile from their village is the jutting bend of Jatrabari village. The men take their boats near there, and lower bamboo poles. Starting from that bend a vast underwater silt bed has formed, stretching far upstream, how far they cannot figure out. They notice that one of the bathers, prompted by the desire for a deep dip, has slowly walked in almost midstream, and is still standing only in neck-high water. For the first time in their lives they see such an amazing thing.

During the rainy season, Titash becomes full to the brim. At the end of the season, the water level goes down and the silt bed reappears above water like a heaved chest. Where has so much water gone! Where has so much fish gone! Only two narrow channels remain flowing near the two shores of Titash, the only evidence that a brimming river once flowed here.[31]

Thus, Adwaita reminds us that the rise in the Titash's silt bed would create a crisis among the fishermen, which what then act as a strong force for migration, compelling the Malos to become 'Environment-induced Displaced Persons' (EIDPs). Since most Malos were not agriculturalists, the silt bed would be cultivated only by peasants. The fishermen living along the Titash would never dream of engaging in agriculture. According to the novelist:

> ... As long as this land was under water, the Malos moved on it, it was theirs. The moment it has floated above water, it has become the farmers'. They will plant seeds here; they will harvest and take home the crop. This right will always stay theirs; no one will be able to steal it. This right of theirs is staked in solid reality, rooted in soil. And the Malos' right was in the flowing water, in its formless, groundless ever-moving fluidity. That right never found the solid touch of real ground, it never had a stable support, a hard foothold. Hence they are the floaters. No matter how much they, the fishermen, befriend the tree and the homes on the ground, they remain floating like vapour. No matter how hard they cling to the bosom of the earth, the soil of the earth is forever pushing them away: 'No space for you, no place for you!' As long as there is water in the river, only that long do they float on the water. When water dries, the too evaporate and disappear.[32]

The Malos living near the Titash could not accept the internal changes in the river that caused water shortages. Thus, they began to migrate to new places as fishing could no longer be their livelihood. Thus, environmental changes created an acute crisis among the Malos. In 1985, El Hinnawi, in a classic study, identified the migration of people due to degradation in the source of their income; this research was in line with what Adwaita had noticed in the 1940s.[33] In his words:

By the end of that year, with summer, the Malos become paralysed. The siltbed has risen close to the banks. Only a thin stream of water is left along the edges, too thin for a fishing boat to move through … Stuck on dry ground under the sun, the fishing boats are cracking; the water in the river is too little to keep them floating. The Malos still have not given up fishing. With the triangular push net on one shoulder and a narrow-neck fish basket on the other, they desperately roam all day from one village to another looking for a pond or a tank. When they spot a clogged pond in some village, they scan it with hawk eyes. Their bodies have become skin and bones, their eyes sunken in their sockets.

Manmohan has throughout the whole day pushed his dip net in one clogged pond after another, but he has found no fish, only frogs. He is back home without rice. Throwing the basket in a corner, he props the net against a fence. His mother has become thin like rope. He married only a few years ago. Without food, his wife is also becoming emaciated. He cannot bear to look at her anymore. His mother and wife both come out of the hut when they hear him come; silently they go back in when they see no bundle of rice in his hand. They all will pass the day without food; they do not know if there will be anything to eat tomorrow either …

Many of the Malo families have left the village. Those who left early on, when there was still water in the river, took their belongings and sections of their huts piled in their boats. Those who went later, left behind their huts and belongings. Those who are still here do not even know where they have gone. Some have gone to harvest paddy for farmers. Some have gone to the side of the big river. There the moneyed folk have arrangements of catching fish on a large scale for their business. The Malos gone there will catch fish in the river on their behalf in exchange for subsistence.

... With fishing in the river disrupted, taken the work offered by the shopkeeper Pals, the job of bringing sacks of goods on their backs from the town to the shop in exchange for a few annas per trip. Carrying those sacks, their spines are so bent that many are no longer able to do even that, and they now stay home waiting for death.[34]

A River Called Titash shows that the Malos of a particular village were forced to migrate to a safer place and take up non-fishing profession(s) because of ecological changes to the source of their livelihood.

Adwaita did not stop here. He further describes the narrative of the crisis faced by the Malos due to environmental change. He illustrates the condition of the Malo women who did not have male member in their family in the following words:

What do they do? ... by gritting their teeth they go away to beg ... But that way is very slippery! Some stumble and fall there, and can never get up to show their face back home. They disappear without a trace from the Malo neighbourhood.

Those who have died are in a way saved. Those who are alive are only wondering, how much longer! From the side of Titash, the answer seems to draft in, not much longer![35]

The concluding part of the novel is heartbreaking. Adwaita writes: 'That Malo neighbourhood is no more. The empty hut-bases are all covered with wild growth. The wind blows through them and makes a rustling sound. Or maybe it's the sighing of those who have fallen and died here.'[36] It appears that the prosperous Malo village vanishes in course of time due to ecological transformations, i.e. rise of the *chars*. *A River Called Titash* is not merely a novel on the Malo fisherfolk; rather, it is a unique example of 'environment-induced crisis migration' in twentieth-century India.

Concluding Observations

Migration is a natural phenomenon of the society, both animal and human. Migration of human populations to avoid harsh seasonal changes, enemies and long-term environmental transformations are being studied from multiple perspectives. 'Environment-induced crisis migration' is, thus, a core theme of environmental discourse. In this context, the literary portrayal of 'nature-induced forced migration' of the Malo fishermen of eastern Bengal, as illustrated by Adwaita Malla Barman, is no doubt innovative. The novel highlights climate-induced displacement in the 1940s, long before the adoption of the UN Guiding Principles on Internal Displacement (2001). It also illustrates the changing eco-morphology of the rivers of Bengal and their relationship with river-dependent communities, such as fishermen. *A River Called Titash* is an extremely relevant novel to understand the nature of environment-induced forced migration of a community. In my opinion, the novel must be assessed as a literary image of EIDPs and seen a document that could help us realize the essence of the UN Guiding Principles on Internal Displacement.

Notes

1. For details about the concept of forced migration, see Essam El-Hinnawi, *Environmental Refugees*, Nairobi: United Nations Environmental Programme, 1985; Richard Bilsborrow and Pamela F. Delargy, *Land Use, Migration and Natural Resource Deterioration: The Experience of Guatemala and Sudan*, Chapel Hill: The University of North Carolina, 1991; Equity and Justice Working Group Bangladesh, *Climate Change Induced Forced Migrants: In Need of Dignified Recognition under a New Protocol,* Dhaka: Equity BD, 2009; Rup Kumar Barman, *Migration, State Polices and Citizenship*, New Delhi: Aayu Publications, 2020.
2. For details see Rup Kumar Barman, *Caste, Class and Culture: The Malos, Adwaita Malla Barman and History of India and Bangladesh*, New Delhi: Abhijeet Publications, 2020.
3. Montgomery Martin, *The History, Antiquities, Topography and Statistics of Eastern India*, 5 vols., 1838; repr., Delhi: Cosmo Publications, 1976.
4. Ibid., vol. V, p. 531.
5. Ibid., vol. III, p. 774.
6. James Wise, *Notes on Race, Castes and Trades of Eastern Bengal*, London: Harrison and Sons, 1883.
7. H.H. Risley, *The Tribes and Castes of Bengal*, vol. II, Calcutta: Firma Mukhopadhyay, 1981, p. 65.
8. For details see Rup Kumar Barman, *Fisheries and Fishermen: A Socio-economic History of Fisheries and Fishermen of Colonial Bengal and Post-colonial West Bengal*, Delhi: Abhijeet Publications, 2008, pp. 13–38.
9. Risley, *Tribes and Castes of Bengal*, vol. II, p. 65.
10. Barman, *Fisheries and Fishermen*, pp. 5–9.
11. Risley, *Tribes and Castes of Bengal*, vol. II, p. 64–5.
12. *Jhal Mal Bandhav* and other literary pieces produced by the Malos (such as Dharmachand Malla Barman,

Sankshipta Kshatriya Tattva, Dacca: Mahesh Chandra Barman, 1923; Dharma Chand Malla Barman, *Sankshipta Jhalla Malla Kshatriya Tattva*, Dacca: Jhalla Malla Samity, 1924; Mahendra Nath Malla Barman, *Dvitiya Barna Kshatriya*, Mymensingh: Sen Brothers Press, 1914, etc.) have described the Malo middle class of the 1920s. For more details, see Rup Kumar Barman and Krishna Kumar Sarkar, eds., *Malo Jatir Itihas O Akar Grantha*, Kolkata, Cognition Publications: 2020.

13. Self-translated from Mahendra Nath Malla Barman, *Jhalla Malla Parichary*, Mymensingh: Sen Brothers Press, 1914, p. 22.
14. Ibid., p. 33.
15. Adwaita Malla Barman, *Titash Ekti Nadir Naam*, tr. Kalpana Bardhan, New Delhi: Penguin, 1992, pp. 7–8 (henceforth *A River Called Titash*).
16. Ibid., pp. 23–4.
17. Ibid, p. 38.
18. Ibid, p. 87.
19. Ibid.
20. Ibid.
21. Self-translated from *Adwaita Malla Barman Rachana Samagra*, ed. Achintya Biswas, Kolkata: Days Publishing, 2000, p. 34.
22. Adwiata Malla Barman's 'Death of Asalata' was first published in 1947 in *Ekal Saradiya*. It has been reprinted in *Bhasaman*, vol. 10, Kolkata: AMBECS, 2010, pp. 1–8.
23. *Adwaita Malla Barman Rachana Samagra*, p. 595.
24. Adwaita Malla Barman: *Bharter Chithi—Pearl Buck ke* (Letter of India—to Pearl Buck), Translated by self, *Adwaita Malla Barman Rachana Samagra*, p. 565.
25. *A River Called Titash*, pp. 14 and 20.
26. Ibid., p. 25.
27. Ibid., p. 6.

28. Ibid., p. 46.
29. Ibid., p. 38
30. Ibid., p. 9
31. Ibid., pp. 259–60
32. Ibid., p. 261.
33. Hinnawi, *Environmental Refugees.*
34. *A River Called Titash*, pp. 269–71.
35. Ibid., pp. 271.
36. Ibid., p. 275.

2

Struggle in the Assam–Bengal River Basins

Fictional Illustrations in Historical Perspective

The growth of civilizations in river basins is a common feature across the history of settled civilizations. From the ancient societies to the present day, river systems have been centres of fishing, agriculture, transport, trade and commerce, and state politics. Thus, rivers can be considered essential living organs of human society. River-basin dweller in different parts of the world have maintained ancient occupations (like fishing, boating and agriculture) in the face of constant ecological disruptions.

The rivers of eastern and north-eastern India (especially Bengal and Assam) are very important to the understanding of the struggles of the people living there. Historians have aspired to conceptualize their problems through multiple perspectives. However, their task is often supplemented by the fictional works left by writers. Unsurprisingly, the rivers of Bengal and Assam have been frequently used by Bengali and Assamese novelists to highlight the tensions of the riverine people of their respective regions. Their struggles for existence, power-politics, socio-cultural traditions and, of course, the question of 'thought control' are unavoidably linked with the river system. In order to historicize the struggle of the people in the river basins of eastern and north-eastern India, I have examined two novels in this chapter. These are: (i) *Tista Parer Brittanta* by Debesh Ray (1988), and (ii) *Kalahi Nadi: Ikul Hikul* by Jitendra Das (1989).

Tistaparer Brittanta: The Struggles of a Region

The prominent rivers of Bengal are closely connected to regional, national and transnational history. The same can be said of the region's internal water bodies and coastal belt. This relationship has been illustrated by Bengali writer in their innumerable creations. In this context, the Tista River has received considerable attention from Bengali writers and social scientists since it has been a focal point of conflicts regarding issues of displacement and construction of barrages. The river is also at the core of a dispute between India and Bangladesh over water-sharing. However, for the people who live in its basin, the Tista is a symbol of culture. All these features, intrinsic to the river, can be understood by analysing an Akademi Award winning Bengali novel *Tistaparer Brittanta* by Debesh Roy. The first part of the novel was published in a periodical called *Baromas* between 1980 and 1981. The second part was published in *Saradiya Kalantar* between 1984 and 1986. The final part of this novel was available in printed form in 1987 in a special issue of *Pratikshan*. The work was finally published as a complete novel in 1988.[1] *Tistaparer Brittanta* deals with the different phases of struggle undertaken by people of the Tista river basin.

The Tista is a transnational river with a total length of 315 km. It has its origin in the eastern Himalayas and flows through Sikkim, Rangpo, Kalimpong, Jalpaiguri and Mekhliganj in West Bengal. It receives the Dik Chhu, the Rangpo, the Lang Lang Chu, the Lachung, the Rani Khola, the Ranghap Chhu, the Rangeet and the Ringyang Chhu as its tributaries. It ultimately joins the Jamuna at Fulchari in Bangladesh.

The Tista is closely associated with different communities and their respective socio-religious cultures. It is a sacred river to communities like the Rajbanshis, the Nepalese, the Lepchas, to name a few.[2] Among such communities, the Rajbanshis live the closest to the Tista and worship the river as their mother. It is a symbol of their prosperity, existence and their culture. Any kind of problem arising in the Tista is, thus, a sign of misfortune.

Roy begins *Tistaparer Brittanta* with a brief description of the people of the Tista basin at Krantihat (Jalpaiguri district, West Bengal). He presents the neighbourhood of Krantihat and its people, including Hindu and Muslim Rajbanshis, tea-garden labourers (especially the Madasias) and the migrants from East Bengal. The novelist mentions that the pre-settled 'Rajbanshi landed class' had faced a critical challenge in the years after Partition as West Bengal was a border state and faced great population pressures from Indian provinces as well as newly established Pakistan. This was especially due to the 'land reforms programme' in West Bengal under the United Front government (1967–9) and later under the Left Front government (1977–2011).[3] Agricultural land has always been a sensitive issue in West Bengal. The large-scale migration of East Bengali minorities (especially of Bengali Hindus) to West Bengal after Partition increased the demand for agricultural land. The problems of resettling East Bengali refugees and voluntary migrants as well as the continuity of a feudal zamindari system added to the issue of land reforms. After the introduction of the Estate Acquisition Act (1953), a large number of Rajbanshi jotedars lost any lands that were in excess of 75 bighas (25 acres). *Khas* or vested land was distributed to the landless cultivators. Although the jotedars were mostly Rajbanshis, many of their fellow caste members were comparatively less lucky. Hence, there was a strong appeal in north Bengal for the distribution of vested land to the Rajbanshis. In 1955, the Siliguri Zonal Kshatriya Samity (SZKS) resolved that:

> in the law made for acquisition and re-distribution of lands, the necessary provision is required to be made by the Govt. of West Bengal so that the lands acquired from Rajbanshi-Kshatriya *Jotdars* of Bengal are distributed among the native cultivators of the locality who mostly belong to the Rajbanshi-Kshatriya community and who are actually landless since long past.[4]

Similar demands were also raised by other Scheduled Caste organizations of north Bengal. Thus, feelings of resentment against non-Rajbanshis began to grow among Rajbanshis in the 1950s. The Rajbanshis of

Cooch Behar demanded 60 per cent reservation in government jobs in order to compensate for the loss of their lands.[5] However, the literacy rate of the Scheduled Castes of Cooch Behar in 1961 was not more than 5.5 per cent while the district average was 29 per cent. Naturally, it was not possible for the Rajbanshis to gain the level of reservation they had originally demanded. Thus, the possession of cultivable lands was the primary means through which the Rajbanshis developed their economic status. Naturally, redistribution of agricultural lands to the non-Rajbanshis sowed contentious ideas of deprivation among the pre-settled communities of the Tista basin. *Tistaparer Brittanta* has illustrated these historical aspects with great care.

The second phase of land reforms was undertaken in West Bengal with the establishment of the United Front (UF) government in 1967. During the period between 1967 and 1969, the UF government vested one million acres of land to non-Ranjbanshis, dismantling the social domination of landed aristocrats (jotedars or zamindars).[6] However, the third phase of land reforms, called 'Operation Burga' under the Left Front (LF) government, was successful in redistributing family land and recorded the creation of 1.2 million sharecroppers within three years (1978–81).[7] According to official sources, 428,180 hectares vested land was distributed among 2,605,432 beneficiaries. In north Bengal 1,70,082 hectares vested land was distributed among 671,841 beneficiaries out of which 301,498 were Scheduled Castes (SC) and 144,184 were Scheduled Tribes (ST) (as shown in the Table 2.1 and Table 2.2).[8]

TABLE 2.1: The Scheduled Castes and Scheduled Tribes Families of North Bengal who Benefitted from Operation Burga

District/ State	*Total figure*	*Scheduled Caste*	*Scheduled Tribes*	*Percentage of SC/ST beneficiaries*
West Bengal	1,346,757	401,617	162,662	41.89
Darjeeling	12,831	4,139	3,028	55.85
Jalpaiguri	55,792	25,769	12,841	51.27
Cooch Behar	74,420	44,507	770	60.83
West Dinajpur	96,431	26,534	28,699	57.27
Maldah	75,453	19,056	18,993	49.10

Source: Department of SC and ST Welfare, Government of West Bengal.

TABLE 2.2: Distribution of Vested Land till 1995

Descriptions	*West Bengal*	*North Bengal*
Distributed vested land	428,179.95 hectares	170,081.80 hectares (39.09 per cent)
Beneficiaries	2,605,432	671,841 (SC 301,491; ST 144,184)
Bargadars	14,98,386	343,817
Land cultivated by sharecroppers	448,286.16 hectares	142,405.26 hectares

Source: Dinesh Dakua, *Kamtapuri Andolon Ekti Jana Bichbhinna Andolan*, Calcutta: National Book Agency, 2003, pp. 30–1

Land reforms and distribution of vested lands to landless agricultural labourers by the UF and the LF governments had a direct impact on the mental framework of the people of the Tista basin. The Uttarkhanda Dal (UKD, 1969) and the Uttarbanga Tapasili Jati O Adibashi Samity (UTJAS, 1977), two prominent socio-political organizations founded by the Rajbanshis, had criticized the government's land reform policy, particularly the mode of redistribution of acquired land to landless cultivators. The UKD and other organizations claimed that the 'East Bengali refugees' were blatantly given preference with regard to land distribution. A feeling of resentment against East Bengalis was thus emerging in the Tista region. The sense of deprivation felt by the landed classes was transformed into a political opportunity.

The above-mentioned episode of land reform and its consequences have been illustrated by Roy in *Tistaparer Brittanta*. The Rajbanshi characters from the landed classes (like Nouchar Alam and Gayanath Jotdar) and their fellow members sensitized the issue of Rajbanshi/Kamtapuri language to protect their feudal rights on their ancestral land. On the other hand, the struggle of the 'East Bengali migrants' as well as the landless agricultural workers and the poor people of the Tista basin have also been illustrated by the novelist in minute detail (which historians of north Bengal studies have failed to illustrate). The representatives of the most marginalized class have a prominent position in *Tista Parer Brittanta*. Characters like Bagharu, Nitai, and Madarir Ma (as well as many other minor characters) have been constructed in such a way that they accurately represent people living in extreme poverty; they are practically considered the slaves of the dominant classes.

Historical studies on 'floods' in prominent river systems have been a major concern among environmental historians for the past few decades. In this context, flooding of the rivers of north Bengal and Assam is an alarming phenomenon for the people inhabiting those areas. The flooding of the Tista is prominently represented in *Tista Parer Brittanta*. As floods, like all natural calamities, do not adhere to international borders, 'flood-induced' displacement' is quite common in both India and Bangladesh as the Tista flows through both countries. Debes Ray has illustrated this environmental phenomenon as well as the consequent 'environment-induced migration' with great care.[9]

Tista Parer Brittanta ends with the construction of a barrage on the Tista in the 1980s. This barrage was much needed for three reasons: (a) flood control, (b) irrigation for agriculture, and (c) supply of water to other rivers. For the Rajbanshi landed class, this barrage is a symbol of interruption to their settled, peaceful lives. Thus, the UKD tried to mobilize the feeling of distress among the Rajbanshis and instigated them to raise their voice for: (a) a separate state in north Bengal called Uttar Khanda or Kamtapur, (b) protection of the Rajbanshi culture, and (c) to stop the construction of the Tista barrage at their expense.[10]

However, the novelist has aptly identified that the Rajbanshis were not united in their protests against state-sponsored development projects. This self-contradiction within the community along class lines did not allow sentiments of regionalism to persist for long. Simultaneously, Roy apprehended that the natural relationship of the people of the Tista basin would change rapidly after the completion of the barrage project. This, however, is a topic of research for future novelists and historians.[11]

Kalahi Nadi Ikul Hikul: The Struggle for Nationhood

Kalahi Nadi: Ikul Hikul (Both Banks of the Kalahi River) is an Assamese novel by Jitendra Das that won an award from the Kamrup Sahitya Parishad in 1988–9. It was published as a complete novel in 1989.[12] Though the title of the novel has been taken from a folk song of the Kalahi river basin of Assam, it illustrates the struggles of the people of the entire state in broader perspective. In the Preface, the novelist confessed that *Kalahi Nadi: Ikul Hikul* is a collection of stories that depict the realities of Assamese society, politics, culture, economy, history, regionalism, folklore, and shared memories.[13]

The novel begins not with any river but with a floodplain lake popularly called '*Deepar Beel*'. Along with a brief historical background of *Deepar Beel*, Das has provided a brief description of the people of this water body. One of the main characters of the novel, a widow named Mahima Bai, is a fisherwoman. She hails from Kukurmara village on the bank of *Deepar Beel*. She and her sons catch fish from the lake as well as from the Kalahi and sells them in the market along with other villagers.[14] Das portrays Mahima Bai as a symbol of the true spirit of Assamese society. She does not 'care' about anyone's opinion. The novelist writes:

Mahima Bai is such a woman who is free from prejudice. She aspires to remain always free. Mahimabai is a self-dependent lady. She knows that beggary is the worst thing of the world. She knows that poverty and sorrows are quite common in life. But Mahimabai does not take them very seriously. She feels proud for rich history and culture of her land.[15]

The central character of the novel is an Assam Civil Servant (ACS), Mr Balin Thakuria (SDC). He also hails from the same locality as Mahima Bai, i.e. the Kalahipar (the basin of the Kalahi River). During his childhood, Balin was brought up by Mahima Bai, who was very caring. The latter knew everything about Balin including his favourite foods and fruits, his dressing style, and his habits.[16]

This close relationship (like that between a mother and child) soon became a dilemma when Balin Thakuria arrested Mahima Bai's kinsmen on the charge of creating disturbance and violating law and order. This disturbance, popularly known as *Bideshi Kheda* (expulsion of foreigners), arose against 'outsiders'. This was a very critical time in Assam. The entire state was engulfed in the *Bideshi Kheda* and *Bangal Kheda* (expulsion of the Bengali) movements, especially in 1979. The novelist explains the background of the student movement of Assam, including the political aspiration of Abida Ahmed (wife of the former President of India, Fakhruddin Ali Ahmed [1974–7]) and its consequences.[17] The people of Assam, especially young students, did not accept Congress-led politics as the party had avoided the issue of expulsion of foreigners from Assam. The assertive voice of the Assamese students, with support from the middle class, led to clashes between student groups and the state police and Central Reserve Police Force (CRPF). This resulted in the death of a large number of students, sparking sentiments of Assamese nationalism.

The novel takes a new turn with this incident. Das gives a detailed description of the *Bideshi Kheda* movement and illustrates sentiments of Assamese nationalism through the following songs:

(A)

O, CRP Hussiar!
O, Bideshi Namaskar!
Karibo je lagibo Sonar Assam pariskar.[18]

(B)

Ejani, unaish unashi san
Assame kare Andolan,
Bideshihire bhare Amar Assam
Nedu Nedu Sonar Ahom.[19]

(A)

Hello! CRPF, be careful.
Ohh! Foreigner, goodbye!
We'll have to clean Golden Assam from you.

(B)

It is 1979; the people of Assam have started a movement.
Entire Assam is full of foreigners.
We'll not hand over our golden Assam to them.

These songs indicate that the people of the Kalahi basin aspired to expel the 'outsiders'. On 23 June

1979, the students of Guwahati University decided to go on an 'All Assam Strike' for this very cause.[20]

The novelist also gives a brief history of the expulsion of the so-called foreigners in the 1960s. He provides this description through the story of a very minor character of the novel, Matibar, who was close to Balin Thakuria and Mahima Bai. Matibar was a member of a Muslim migrant family from East Pakistan. He, along with his family and other migrants from East Pakistan, were expelled from the Kalahi basin in 1962. Das, thus, discusses the large-scale migration of Bengali Muslim cultivators from East Bengal to Assam and its consequences before and after Indian Independence in 1947. Concurrently, he also delves into the settlement of Nepalis and Punjabis in Assam (including in the Kalahi basin). He has aptly illustrated the Kalahi basin as symbolic of 'mini-India'. Therefore, the novelist has raised a very serious question about the meaning of 'outsider' in the context of Assam. The central character of this novel, Balin Thakuria, thinks that the people who were born and brought up in Assam and have contributed to the region's struggles are Assamese! They should not be considered 'outsiders' at any cost.

However, the novelist has illustrated a different picture regarding the 'Bengali-speaking people' of the Kachar region of Assam (popularly called the *Bangali/Bangal* or *Siloittya Bangali*). He writes: 'The Bengalis despite living in Assam are not interested to acquire the knowledge of the Assamese language.'[21] On the other hand, he also describes in details the background of the language movement of the 'Bengali speaking people' of Assam. The novelist is conscious about the inherent differences between the Assamese and the Bengalis. He gives examples of how two persons—one Assamese, one Bengali—in the Kalahi basin were subjected to a miserable death 'only for linguistic difference'.[22] The young Bengali man was brutally murdered by the Assamese merely because he was a Bengali while the Assamese man was tortured by the Bengalis to such an extent that he lost his eyes and later committed suicide.[23] The Assamese man in the novel turns out to be Mahima Bai's husband.

The novel *Kalahi Nadi* occasionally deals with the growth of the Communist movement in Assam, including the story of Bishnu Prasad Rabha (1909–69). The nexus between the business class and government servants and the suffering masses contributed to the growth of a pro-Communist feeling in the region. Thus, the economic struggle of the working class, peasantry and the tribal people of the Kalahi basin is given a prominent place in the novel. On the whole, the novelist presents the struggle of the communities in the Kalahi basin from multiple perspectives:

(a) The Assamese people (especially the educated middle class) were very much concerned about the question of domination by the so-called 'outsiders/foreigners/*bideshi*'.
(b) 'The Bengali speaking people' were more concerned about their 'identity' including their language and culture.
(c) The landed and politically dominant Assamese were more interested in their political future.

(d) The common people of Assam were conscious about economic exploitation and their own suffering.

This complex situation turned violent when the All Assam Student Union (AASU) called for an 'Assam strike' in 1979. This, as well as internal contractions among the political elites eventually ended with the death of Mahima Bai at the hands of the police. Balin Thakuria observes that her death appears to be a matter of political capital for both the supporters of the Congress (I) and the followers of the Assam movement. The situation grew even more complex when Balin Thakuria was charged with the death of Mahima Bai, leading to him being attacked by a crowd of people. What was he to do? Should he resign from government service or issue on order to arresting his assailants? Das raises these questions and asks readers to search for their answers.

Concluding Observations

Tistaparer Brittanta and *Kalahi Nadi: Ikul Hikul* are political novels. In both, rivers have been used as symbols of people's political aspirations. Both novels were written to understand the aspirations and contradictions of the people of north Bengal and Assam, respectively (especially during the critical periods of the 1970s and 1980s). Both Roy and Das have depicted rivers as markers of 'community' and 'nationality'. However, these novels are equally important in making people understand the environmental history of both northern Bengal and Assam.

One common feature of these novels is the 'land question'. Questions of land ownership, modes of agricultural operation, continuity of semi-feudal systems and exploitation of 'labour value' are essentially linked with traditions, climate, and the quality of soil. Both Roy and Das have argued that the regions under study had remained backward under the precolonial and colonial states. However, the colonial state apparatus for exploiting forests, wild animals, rivers, and other natural resources as well as the mechanism for maximizing revenue developed to a great extent in these two regions. This trend contributed to the migration of people from different corners of India to these regions. However, this growth was considered tolerable till 1947.

Population overflow appeared to be a very serious problem after 1947 especially due to 'conflict-induced migration' from East Pakistan. The new migrants were initially received by the 'hosts' with great care and sympathy. However, the hosts soon felt that newcomers had become their enemies as the latter had supposedly established dominance in every aspect of life (including education, culture, economy, and politics). Both the West Bengal and Assam governments did not take this problem very seriously. Naturally, the pre-settled communities (like the Rajbanshis of north Bengal and the Assamese) were looking for redressal of their material and cultural problem under the *Bideshi Kheda* movement. Thus the 'Assam movement' and 'the Kamtapuri/ Uttarkhand movement' received considerable attention from poor people, the educated middle class, and the declining landed class. The Communists were in a dilemma. In

West Bengal, the Left Front government had remained in power only through the distribution of land to marginalized groups.

Thus, a broader perspective of the conflict-ridden 1970s and 1980s has been illustrated by the novelists. Both writers were familiar with the complexity of the movement to expel 'outsiders' and had close relations with the character archetypes in their works. They used the local language (Kamtapuri/ Rajbanshi by Roy and south Kamrupi by Das) and depicted local traditions, folklore, history, and cultural features to present the people of the Tista and Kalahi basins, respectively, within the broader context of Indian society. In fact, both identified the Tista and the Kalahi basins to be a 'mini India'. Thus, it appears that the Tista and the Kalahi are not merely rivers! They symbolized the history of their people (material, social, cultural and, of course, political) and had withstood a number of the political and economic developments (including the construction of dams, barrages, bridges, and canals). Though the novelist of *Kalahi Nadi: Ikul Hikul* did not give readers an answer regarding the consequences of the developments in the Kalahipar, Roy indicated the developments that took place in the post-barrage life of people from the Tista basin.

Notes

1. Debes Roy, *Tistaparer Brittanta* (henceforth *Tista Parer Brittanta*), 16th edn., Kolkata: Dey's Publishing, 2013, p. i.
2. For details see Abhijeet Das, *Tista: Utsa theke Mohana*, Kolkata: Ekhon Duars, 2019.

3. For details see D. Bandyopadhaya, 'Land Reforms in West Bengal: Remembering Harekrishna Konar and Benoy Choudhury, *Economic and Political Weekly*, vol. XXXV, no. 21, 2000.
4. *Proceedings of the First Annual Conference of the Siliguri Zonal Kshatriya Samity, dated 8th April 1955*, Siliguri: Siliguri Kshatriya Samity, 1955, p. ii.
5. *Memorandum Submitted to the Scheduled Caste and Scheduled Tribe Commission by the Cooch Behar District Depressed Classes League, dated 29th April 1961*, Cooch Behar: Cooch Behar Depressed Classes League, 1961, p. i.
6. Bandyopadhaya, 'Land Reforms in West Bengal', p. 1796.
7. Ibid., p. 1797.
8. Government of West Bengal, *Hataman Jara Tulechhe Shir*, Calcutta: Department of SC and ST, 1987, p. 7; Dinesh Dakua, *Kamtapuri Andolon Ekti Jana Bichhinna Andolan*, Calcutta: National Book Agency, 2003, pp. 30–1.
9. *Tista Parer Brittanta*, p. 268.
10. Ibid., p. 431.
11. Ibid., pp. 495–504.
12. Jitendra Das, *Kalahi Nadi: Ikul Hikul*, Guwahati: Chandra Prakash: 1989, p. i.
13. Ibid., p. ii.
14. Mahima Bai's husband was tortured by the Bengali-speaking people as a form of revenge and due to the anti-Bengali feeling among the Assamese in the 1960s. The Assamese–Bengali riots and the attitude of the Assam government had a disruptive impact on the people of Chhaygaon, the region in which the novel takes place.
15. Das, *Kalahi Nadi*, p. 7.
16. Ibid., pp. 11–13.
17. On the eve of the election of 1979, the movement took a serious in Assam. In Barpeta constituency, a young

leader, Khageswar Talukdar, was brutally tortured by the police and then later found dead. He was recognized as the 'first martyr of the Assam movement'. Ibid., p. 17.

18. Ibid., p. 22. Translated by the author.
19. Ibid., p. 26. Translated by the author.
20. Ibid., p. 19.
21. Ibid., p. 64.
22. Ibid., p. 70.
23. Ibid.

3

From Wang Chhu to Raidak

Reflections on the Society and Culture of River Basins

Can we imagine the history and cultural heritage of the Indian subcontinent without its rivers? It is evident to historians that the 'chain of rivers and their basins are inseparably attached with the historical evolution of India and its neighbouring countries'. In fact, the rivers of South Asia are considered 'sacred' and the 'mother of civilization'. They are peoples' guides, sources of livelihood, trade, commerce, and transport and are integral to regional production systems and the national economy. Thus, they are intrinsic to the religion, culture, language, and the national identity of a country.

South Asian rivers have diverse characters in terms of their origin, courses, and ecological importance. However, due to the indiscriminate discharge of industrial pollutants, garbage, and waste from urban centres, many rivers have dried up. In fact, many of them have been transformed into mythological conceptualization. However, historians, social scientists, engineers, politicians, and policy-makers are extremely concerned about this issue. Naturally, innumerable works of research have been produced in the context of South Asia. Starting from the Brahmaputra in the east to the Indus in the west, and from the Ganga–Jamuna from the north to the Krishna, Kavery, Godavari, and Narmada in the south, the rivers of the Indian subcontinent have been studied from multiple perspectives. However, there are many rivers that have not received adequate attention from scholars engaged in nationalist discourse, cultural studies, and international politics and policies. Among such streams, the Raidak is a notable transnational river that is linked with the history and cultural heritage of Bhutan, India, and Bangladesh. In this chapter, a humble attempt has been made to present and include the Raidak in the discourse of environmental studies .

Society and Culture of the *Wang Chhu* Basin

The Raidak is a transnational river. It originates in the Himalayas in Bhutan, where it is called the Wang Chhu.[1] The Wang Chhu and the Paro Chhu meet near Thimphu and together form the Thimphu Chhu. The Wang Chhu also has two tributaries above the Paro Dzong: the Ta Chhu (from the east) and the Ha Chhu (from the west). The Wang Chhu flows from Thimphu to the Indo-Bhutan border as a very rapid stream and is connected to the natural history of Bhutan. Beginning from the Jigme Dorj National Park in the north to Phipsoo Wildlife Sanctuary in the south, the deep forests of the Wang Chhu basin are rich in a variety of Himalayan flora and fauna.

The Wang Chhu is considered the 'lifeline' of national economy of Bhutan. Thimphu, the country's capital is located on its banks. The city is connected to Paro and Phuentsholling through the highway passing along the Wang Chhu. As a hill stream around 2,121 m. above sea level (6,959 ft.), the Wang Chhu is a source of water, boulders, and stones. These natural resources have immense value in the Bhutanese economy. Boulders of the Wang Chhu basin are in gret demand in the country's cement industry. In fact, boulders, dolemite and stones from the Wang Chhu region are regularly exported to Bangladesh on a large scale. Just a few kilometres downhill from the confluence of the Ha Chhu and the Wang Chhu, the Bhutan government began the construction of the Chukha Hydro-Electric Project in 1974 (with India's financial and technical assistance). It was completed in 1986–8 and had a capacity of 336 MW. Bhutan has constructed another 'run of the river type hydro-electric at Tala', just 3 km. downstream from the Chukha Project. This has been generating electricity since 2007 with a capacity of 1,020 MW.

The Chukha power projects on the Wang Chhu fostered the economic development of the district. Chukha (with its headquarters at Phuentsholing, bordering India) has emerged as the commercial and financial capital of Bhutan. Thus, this *dzongkhag* (district), hosting some of Bhutan's old industrial companies (like Bhutan Carbide Chemical Limited

[BCCL], Bhutan Boards Products Limited [BBPL] etc.) generates the majority of the GDP of this 'land locked Himalayan country'.

The Wang Chhu and its tributaries have always been regarded as important cultural markers in Bhutan. Religious, linguistic, ethnic, and caste communities are closely attached to the river. Though the total population of Bhutan is less than 1 million, society is immensely pluralistic. There are mainly four major ethnic groups in Bhutan: the Ngalongs (Tibeto-Mongoloids), Sharchops (Indo-Mongoloids), Khengs (earliest inhabitants) and the Lhotshampas (people of Nepali origin). The Ngalongs and the Sharchops constitute the majority, making up around 50 per cent of the total population. Among the Ngalongs, the Drukpas are a majority group who are largely concentrated in western Bhutan along the course of the Wang Chhu. They migrated to Bhutan from Tibet in the ninth and tenth centuries. Most of the ruling elites of Bhutan belong to this community. They are the followers of the Drukpa Kagyu sect of Buddhism. With their social institutions and Dzongkha language, the cultural features of the Drukpas have developed into the 'mainstream culture of Bhutan'.

In Bhutan, the Kagyu sect of Tibetan Buddhism (Lamaism) established several gumphas (monasteries) and dzongs (monastery in a fortress) in the Wang Chhu basin. The dzongs (like Rinpung Dzong and Tashichho Dzong) are very influential among Tibetan Buddhists of the Drukpa lineage. The Rinpung Dzong (also called Paro Dzong) was originally built in the fifteenth century by Drung Drung Gyal and was previously known as Hengrel Dzong. However, it was rebuilt in 1644–6 and came to be known as Rinpung Dzong.[2] The monastic body and the administrative offices of Paro district are located here.

The Tashichho Dzong is located at the northern edge of Thimpu. This monastery was referred to as Tassisudon in the British-Indian administrative reports.[3] The original dzong was established in 1216 by Lama Gyaa Lhanapa; it was rebuilt in 1641 by Ngawang Namgyal and renamed Tashichho Dzong. Even after this, the dzong was damaged several times due to fires and earthquakes. The present structure was built by King Jigme Dorji Wangchuk (1952–72), the third king of the Wangchhuk dynasty. The Tashichho Dzong has been the summer capital of Bhutan for a long time. It is also the seat of the Royal Government of Bhutan. There are several temples, chapels, and shrines within the monastery. The dzongs along the Wang Chhu and its tributaries are thus closely interrelated with the cultural heritage of Bhutan. It is perhaps almost impossible for a Bhutanese of the Kagyu sect to consider religious life without the Wang Chhu.

Bhutan has paid adequate attention to the preservation of the 'cultural heritage' of the Wang Chhu basin. It consider cultural preservation 'a positive and essential means to safeguard national security' by infusing national feeling among the Bhutanese. Thus, Bhutan founded a National Council for Social Cultural Promotion in 1980, the main objectives of which are: (a) organization and promotion of social, cultural, and educational activities to foster and strengthen a feeling of national community transcending regional loyalties; (b) adoption of schemes to develop a sense of national identity among youths and make them dedicate their service to the king and the country; and (c) initiations of plans/programmes calculated to emphasize social, cultural, and spiritual aspects of life and to make the youth participate in activities conducive to national development at the rural level.

In 1986, Bhutan has established a Special Commission for Cultural Affairs. During this time, the country was following a policy of renovating old dzongs (fort), monasteries and chhortens. Dzongkha, the language of the Drukpas, was developed as the national language. The Dzongkha Advisory Board was entrusted to produce Dzongkha textbooks from the pre-primary to the degree levels. Dzongkha became compulsory for elementary education. Bhutan also adopted a 'code of conduct' called *Driglam Namza* (or One Nation, One People). Traditional forms of address for Drukpas—*gho* (for men) and *kira* (for women)—were made compulsory for the Bhutanese. These policies of the Royal Government of Bhutan fostered the spirit of Bhutanese cultural nationalism. Naturally, the culture of the people of the Wang Chhu basin eventually transformed into the national culture of Bhutan.

The Journey of Two Raidaks and the Dudhkumar

The Wang Chhu enters the Alipurduar district of West Bengal (India) through Bhutanghat as a river called the Raidak. The latter is divided into two branches at Tiyamari (Raidak Forest) known as Raidak I and Raidak II. From Tiyamari, the Raidak II flows southwards through the Newland Tea Garden and the villages of Kumargram CD Block. It crosses National Highway 31C at Chakchoka. Just 2 km. downstream from NH31C, the Raidak II enters Cooch Behar district. After flowing through the villages of Tufanganj subdivision, the Raidak II meets the Sankosh River at Bainyaguri (near Boxirhat, Cooch Behar). From Bhutanghat to Bainyaguri, the Raidak II is approximately 50 km. in length.

The combined courses of the Raidak II and the Sankosh enter Assam at Bara Laukuthi (Boxirhat), forming a natural boundary between West Bengal and Assam (from Kumargram to Boxirhat). From Bara Laukuthi, the Sankosh is known as Gangadhar, a notable river of Assam. After flowing through Tamarhat, Agamoni, and Golokganj, the Gangadhar enters Bangladesh and eventually meets the Brahmaputra. Thus, the Raidak II is an essential part of the Brahmaputra system along the Indo–Bangladesh border.

On the other hand, the upper part of the Raidak I (from Tiyamari to the Chipra Beat (an office of the Forest Department, Government of West Bengal) has been recorded as the Dhowlajhora. This river flows through the Raidak Forest, tea gardens, and Baro Chowkir Bos village of Alipurduar CD Block II. It meets a branch of the Raidak near the Chipra Beat. It also receives another river at this point called the Ultanadi (a small river originating from the Raidak II at Lalchandpur, near Kumargram), which is, in turn, connected to the Bara Beel, a floodplain lake located in a nearby forest Nararthali Beat. Thus, the collective courses of the Dhowlajhora, a branch of the Raidak and the Ultanadi, transforms into the Raidak I proper at Sadhur Ashram, the meeting point of the Chipra Beat and Nararthali Beat. From the Raidak Forest to the Chipra Beat, 'the Dhowlajhora-Raidak I' basin abounds with the forests of the Raidak Range under the Buxa Tiger Reserve (BTR).

The following part of the Raidak I's course, i.e. from Chipra Beat to NH31C, is fairly rich in biodiversity. There are two forest settlements along this part of the river: (a) Chipra Beat Rabha Basti on the left bank of the Dhowlajhora,[4] and (b) Madasia (or Adibashi] Basti on the left bank of the Raidak I).[5] However, there is no forest in the right bank of the Raidak I from the Chipra Beat to the NH31C. Rather, there are a few villages of Alipurduar CD Block II.

The Raidak I, from the Raidak Bridge at Purba Chepani and the Raidak Railway Bridge under the NF Railway, flows southwards. After crossing villages of Alipurduar district, the Raidak I enters Tufanganj subdivision of Cooch Behar district. The river then flows gently through Tufanganj subdivision and crosses the NH31A at the town of Tufanganj.

From the NH31 to the Indo-Bangladesh border at Balabhut, the Raidak I is comparatively bigger in size and navigable almost throughout the year. It is because of its navigability that Tufanganj (erstwhile Phulbari) emerged as a prosperous town from the late sixteenth century. From Tufanganj, the Raidak I flows southwards through the densely populated villages of Assam. Balabhut Bridge over the Raidak I has created a link between West Bengal and Assam near the Indo-Bangladesh border. Just below this bridge, the Raidak I receives a tributary called the Gangadhar on its right side.[6] The joint courses of the Raidak and the Gangadhar meet the Dudhkumar River at Char Balabhut village near the Indo-Bangladesh border.

The Dudhkumar is one of the most notable transnational rivers of India and Bangladesh. There are a few Indian villages on its left bank, such as Char Balabhut (West Bengal), Jhaukuthi Jhapushabari (in Dhubri, Assam), Ramraikuthi, and Satrasal (Dhubri district of Assam)]. At Jhaukuthi village, the Dudhkumar enters Bangladesh.[7] From Char Balabhut to the confluence of the Dudhkumar and the Brahmaputra near Nunkhaowa village (Nageswari, Kurigram, Bangladesh), the Dudhkumar flows through the Bhurungamari and Nageswari subdistricts of Kurigram. Bangladesh initiated the construction of the 650 m. long Sonahat Bridge over the Dudhkumar in 2019.

The Raidaks (Raidak I and Raidak II) have created several water bodies by changing their courses. These water bodies are the essential parts of ecology of Alipurduar and Cooch Behar districts of West Bengal, Dhubri district of Assam and Kurigram district of Bangladesh. Like their parent rivers, these water bodies are equally important for the people of the Raidak-Dudhkumar-Sankosh-Gangadhar-Brahmaputra system.

The People of the Raidak Basin

The land between two Raidaks is unique in its social composition. This basin is home to diverse populations from several corners of the Indian subcontinent. The early settlers of the Raidak basin were predominantly indigenous people. Vernacular and Sanskrit texts, Persian literatures and archaeological evidences have left us information about the precolonial societal format of the Raidak basin (comprising multilingual indigenous and non-tribal communities). The *Kalika Purana* has categorically recorded the indigenous people of the region as *kiratas* or *mlechhas*.[8] The *Yogini Tantra* has pronounced them to be *kuvachaka* (evil speakers) or non-Aryan people.[9] Tribal culture and non-Aryan physiques, as illustrated in these texts, indicate the existence of Mongoloid tribal communities in the Raidak basin. The account of Xuanzang (Hiuen Tsiang, 602–64), a Chinese traveller, also recorded the presence of non-Aryan and non-Buddhist populations in the Dudhkumar-Gangadhar-Brahmaputra basin.[10] A similar account has also been documented in the *Tabaqat-i-Nasiri*, a thirteenth century Persian work by Minhaj-ud-din Siraj.[11] Thus, precolonial literature point towards the settlement of indigenous communities, such as the Koches (now Rajbanshis), Meches (Bodos), Rabhas, etc., in the land between the two Raidaks.

The Meches (also known as the Bodos, Boros, or Kacharis) are people of Mongoloid origin living in the Duars region of West Bengal. They are scattered extensively across the basin of the two Raidaks. Like the Meches, the Rabhas are also indigenous people of the Raidak basin. They are also of Mongoloid origin and are main concentrated in Assam and along the Assam–Meghalaya border. In West Bengal, they are mainly distributed along the Raidak basin of Alipurduar and Cooch Behar districts.

The largest indigenous community of the

Raidak basin are the Rajbanshis or Koches. A large population is found in the Raidak basin from Kumargram (Alipurduar) to Kurigram (Bangladesh) and from Bara Laukuthi to Satrasal (Assam). At present, the Rajbanshis constitute the numerically largest Scheduled Caste community of West Bengal (population 38,01,677 in 2011). They are mainly distributed in the northern districts of West Bengal (total 30,67,781, i.e. 80.69 per cent). They are also found, in large numbers, in Assam, Bihar, Bangladesh, and Nepal.

A considerable population of the Rajbanshis along the lower part of the Raidak I and Raidak II have embraced Islam. They are called 'Nashyas' or 'Nashya Sheikhs'. Dense populations of this community are found in almost all villages from Shalbari to Balabhut along the Raidak I. They also live along the Indo-Bangladesh border at Dudhkumar-Gangadhar, particularly in Balabhut (West Bengal) and Satrasal, Kaldoba, and Agamony (Assam).

Sub-Himalayan Bengal (or the western Duars) experienced considerable changes in its social composition from the latter half of nineteenth century due to colonial intervention. The growth of tea gardens near the Raidak I-Dhowlajhora-Chuniajhora-Turturi-Raidak II drainage system attracted low-price workers (called coolies) in droves from the Chhotonagpur region. Workers from Santal, Munda, Malpaharia, Mahali, Lohar, Birhor, Asura, and other tribal communities (present-day Scheduled Tribes) were brought to this region to clear jungles and develop tea plantations. Alongside the tea labourers of Assam and other districts of West Bengal, the workers in this region have gradually emerged as notable tribal communities.

There are several villages along the Raidak basin, where considerable concentrations of Nepali-speaking people are found. They migrated here mainly from eastern Nepal and the hilly regions of West Bengal in the late nineteenth and early twentieth centuries. With the growth of 'colonial mode of production' in the Raidak basin, particularly the growth of tea gardens as well as the extension of agricultural activities, the Nepali settlement began to grow. In the late twentieth century, many Nepalis migrated to the upper part of the Raidak II basin from southern Bhutan.

The Raidak basin has also received people from different corners of the Indian subcontinent. During the colonial period, the Cooch Behar State had invited a considerable number of workers, traders, scholars and administrators from different parts of India. Many of them had settled in the Raidak basin under Tufanganj Subdivision. However, the Raidak basin has received a huge number of people from East Bengal after 1947 as 'forced' and 'voluntary migrants'. This basin has eventually transformed into a region with huge population of East Bengal origin. The East Bengalis are divided into a number caste and occupational communities like the Malos [fishermen], Patnis [boatmen], Yoginaths [a cultivating and weaver caste], Namasudras [former Chandals], Dhobas [washer men], Barujibis [betel leaf cultivators], Mahishyas [a mixed caste of respectable status mainly engaged in agricultural works], Modaks [sweet makers], Jeliya Kaibartyas [fishermen], trading castes [Sahas, Pauls, Baniks], Kamars [Blacksmith], Kumars [potters],

Goyalas [milkmen], Kayasthyas, Brahmins, etc. The Raidak basin has also received a considerable of the Rajbanshis from East Bengal [erstwhile East Pakistan now Bangladesh].

Cultural Life in the Raidak Basin

I have already mentioned how the Wang Chhu is a cultural marker of Bhutan. Like Bhutan, the courses of the Raidak I and Raidak II embody certain specific cultural traditions. It is because of the rivers' geographical and cultural proximity with Bhutan that a few Buddhist families live in the Raidak-I-Dhowlajhora-Raidak II basin. There is a Buddhist monastery at Kumargram near the Raidak II basin. Though not in high concentrations, these Buddhist families also in the upper part of the Raidak basin, particularly near the tea gardens and Samuktala market.

It is evident that Hindu culture is more prominent in the middle and lower part of the Raidak basin. Literary and archeological sources suggest that the Indo-Aryan religious culture emerged in the Tista-Brahmaputra region (including the Raidak basin) in ancient period. The traditions of granting rent-free land to brahmins as well as the construction of temples for Hindu deities by the ruling houses were common in the Pragjyotisha-Kamarupa-Kamata region. These traditions flourished mainly due to the legitimization the ruling families; it is important to note that these ruling house had tribal origins. This trend reached its height with the emergence of the Koches as the ruling power of the Tista-Brahmaputra region.

To legitimize their rule over the multi-ethnic Tista-Brahmaputra valley, the Koch rulers (1515–1949) adopted Indo-Aryan culture—including the construction and maintenance of Hindu temples—as well as propagated its spread. The trend of temple-building began with the foundation of the Kamakshya Temple at Nilachal Hill (Guwahati) by King Naranarayan (1540–87) and Chilarai (commander of the Koch Army). They appointed brahmin priests to the temples and granted huge amounts of *brahmattar* (land donated to brahmins) and *devottar* (land donated to the temple) for its maintenance.[12]

However, the fictitious stories and myths as propagated by the priests of the Kamakshya Temple discouraged the Koch kings and their family members from visiting this temple. In my fieldwork, I noticed the presence of a Kamakshya Dham (seat of Kamakshya) at the bank of the river Mara Raidak called 'Adi Kamakshya Dham' (original site of Kamakshya). It is located at Dakshin Kamakshyaguri village. King Naranarayan and Chilarai also constructed several Shaivite temples across their kingdom, including in the Raidak basin.

Among the Shiva temples constructed by the Koch kings in the Raidak basin, the Chhoto Mahadeva at Nakkati Gachh and Bara Mahadeva at Baro Kodali are notable. These temples had a great influence on the common masses. It is important to note that Shaivism had deep roots in the land prior to the rise of the Koch Kingdom. A popular tribal deity called Bathou (of the *mlechhas*) is identical with Shiva from the Hindu pantheon. In fact, 'Lord Shiva' was the chief deity of the Koch Kingdom. Construction and maintenance of the Shiva temple and appointment of brahmins as priests and tribals as *deories* (tribal priest) accelerated the process of cultural synthesis in the Raidak basin.

However, the Raidak basin was highly influenced by the form of Vaishnavism propagated by Sankaradeva (1449–1568). Sankaradeva was born and brought up in a Bhuiyan family at Alipukuri in Baradowa (present-day Nawgaon district of Assam), which was part of the Ahom Kingdom. But the anti-Bhuiyan policy of the Ahom king Suhungmung Dihingia Raja (1497–1539) compelled him to take shelter in Patboushi village in Barpeta (located within the Koch Kingdom, near the Brahmaputra).[13] A matrimonial alliance was established between the Koch ruling family and that of Sankaradeva. This marriage proved to be very positive as it brought about cultural homogeneity in the kingdom.[14]

The Koch general Chilarai and his wives became Sankaradeva's disciples.[15] The king greatly admired Sankardeva and granted him the *mahal* (revenue-yielding tract) of Barpeta. The Koch kings also supported the construction of several satras (monasteries) and namgharas (Vaishnava prayer halls) across their kingdom, including Cooch Behar, Phulbari (Tufanganj), Dhubri, Goalpara, Satrasal, and Barpeta. The Charita Puthis (biographies of Sankaradeva and his disciples) mention the existence of a large number of satras in the Koch Kingdom.[16] In this context, we must mention these satras flourished in the Raidak basin, particularly Phulbari and its vicinity.

Phulbari (present-day Tufanganj), a notable centre of political power (with a fort constructed by Chilarai called Chilarai Kote), emerged as a seat of

Vaishnavite culture. Several state-patronized satras were established in the Raidak basin such as Kuthibari Satra, Haripur Satra, Madhpur Satra, and Ramraikuthi Satra. The Ramraikuthi Satra is located on the left bank of the Raidak I near the Indo-Bangladesh border at Satrasal (a village in Dhubri district, Assam). It was established by Jagadanada or Ramrai, cousin of Srimanta Sankardeva, in the mid-sixteenth century. Chilarai, the general of the Koch army and brother of King Naranarayan, had married Bhubaneswari, one of Ramraj's daughters. The Charita Puthis have recorded that Sankaradeva (with his 120 disciples and his niece Bhubaneswari) had travelled to Satrasal from Patbausi across the Brahmaputra and laid the foundation of the Ramraikuthi Satra.[17] After this marriage, King Naranarayan donated 1300 bighas of land to this satra for its maintenance.

Haripur Satra (at Nangalgram in Tufanganj), on the other land, was established by Harihar Ata, a notable disciple of Sankaradeva. In fact, there were four other notable satras along the Raidak basin at Tufanganj: Phulbari Satra, Kuthibari Satra, Madhpur Satra, and Dolgobinda Dham. These satras are no longer traceable due to changes in the course of the Raidak I. However, the Haripur Satra was restructured in 1912.

In the late sixteenth and seventeenth centuries, a few satras were established along the Raidak I and Raidak II. Among them, Shalbari Satra (at Shalbari, Tufanganj on the Raidak I), Kamakshyaguri Satra (on the Mara Raidak, Kamakshyaguri), and Nakarkhana Satra (at Bhanukumari, Boxirhat on the Raidak II) are prominent examples.[18] These satras were also founded by Harihar Ata. Though we could not trace any

Vaishnava satra at Kamakshyaguri, a temple called Haribari can be found in Kamakshyaguri market on the banks of the Mara Raidak. Similarly, the Shalbari Satra cannot be traced though there are several families bearing the surname 'Bhakat', a common surname of the followers of Vaishnavism propagated by Srimanta Sankardeva. However, the Nakarkhana Satra still exists to this day. In essence, we can get an idea about the satras established by Harihar Ata from the very names of places and temples in the Raidak basin (like Haribari, Haripur, Haripur Market, etc.).

The Vaishnava satras of the Raidak basin had an intense impact on the Koches and Rabhas, many of whom embraced the religion. The satras, as centres of mass gatherings, had developed a kind of social cohesiveness among the Vaishnavas, imbuing them with a common identity. Thus, the building of neo-Vaishnavite institutions at the cost of the state enhanced indirect state control on the followers of Vaishnavism. Vaishnavism, on the other hand, also influenced the Koch administration. Due to this impact, the Koch rulers assumed the title of 'Narayan' and their coins came to be known as *narayani tanka*.

However, the form of Vaishnavism popular in Bengal had been prioritized in the Koch Kingdom since the eighteenth century. This is made clear in the building of temples in honour of of Madan Mohun (Vishnu). Unsurprisingly, a temple of Modam Mohun was established in Tufanganj, on the banks of the Raidak I. This temple is now a prominent cultural centre of Tufanganj.

The Hindu culture of the Raidak basin further evolved in the postcolonial period with the mass migration of people from eastern and southern Bengal. The upper and middle parts of the Raidak I (particularly from Chhoto Chowkir Bos to the Indo–Bangladesh border) are populated with people from East Bengal who are the followers of Hinduism. They introduced several new cultural traditions relating to rivers (worshiping the Raidak as Mother Ganga) as well as the traditions of worshiping Kartik, Manasha, Swaraswati, Durga, Kali, Shani and Mangal Chandi in the East Bengali style.

Apart from the East Bengali Hindus, the Rajbanshis (both of East Bengali and native origin) follow several Hindu traditions that are specific to their community. Among such cultural traditions, worshipping Mahadeva (Lord Shiva), Bishahari (Goddess Manasha/snake worship), Bhandani and many other local deities and spirits (called Masan Deo) along with certain agriculture-based festivals are significant. At the same time, they often attempted to pacify certain spirits who were considered responsible for the outbreak of diseases. However, the Rajbanshis of the Raidak basin had given up many of their own traditions due to the cultural influence of the non-Rajbanshis.

Another noticeable feature of religious life of Hindus in the Raidak basin was the growth of organized missions like the International Society for Krishna Consciousness (ISKCON), founded in 1966 in USA by A.C. Bhakti Vedanta Swami Prabhupada. From the 1980s, the preachers of Krishna bhakti (devotion to Lord Krishna) encouraged the villagers of Chhoto Chowkir Bos to embrace ISKCON. However, we have also noticed the popularity of certain other religious sects in the Indian part of the Raidak basin, including the Ramakrishna Mission, traditional Vaishnavism, the cult of Anukul Thakur (the Satsangha Cult based out of Deoghar, Jharkhand), and the folk tradition of animism. However, the most common festival in the Raidak river basin is Durga Puja. The Raidak is where Durga and other idols are immersed.

Like other parts of Bengal, Christianity was introduced to the Raidak basin after the colonization of the region and became a prominent religion mainly among indigenous communities, particularly in the tea gardens of the upper basins of the Raidak I and Raidak II. The Christians (and mainly Scottish) missionaries had shown interest in converting the tribal communities of Santalpur (named after the Santal migrants from Bihar and Jharkhand), Mahakalguri, and Khoyardanga since the late nineteenth century. The foundation of a missionary school in Mahakalguri (in 1911) and Santalpur Christian Colony (1890) with several churches became a turning point for conversion of the Meches and other tribal communities. Thus, most of the Meches of Baro Chowkir Bos, Mahakalguri, Uttar Mahakalguri and other nearby villages (located near the Raidak basin) embraced Christianity.[19] The Santalpur Mission also converted the tea-garden workers to Christianity. Along with the tea-garden tribes and the Meches, it has also been discovered that the Rabhas of Chipra Beat Rabha Basti have embraced Christianity in recent years (the twenty-first century). The growth of Christianity in the Raidak basin was a marker of cultural change as well as, more precisely, a tool for the educational development of regional populations. With their conversion to Christianity, these communities came into contact with Western knowledge systems and discarded many of their allegedly 'evil' indigenous practices and customs.

Like Buddhists, Christians, and Hindus, Muslims also established their settlements along the courses of the Raidak and the Dudhkumar. In fact, the indigenous people of this region (particularly the Koches and Meches) have embraced Islam since the thirteenth century. The *Tabaqat-i-Nasiri* recorded the conversion of a Mech chief named Ali Mech into Islam.[20] In fact, the descendants of the early Muslims of this locality still live in Chepani, Dakshin Mahakalguri, and Majidkhana (Masjitkhana) on the western bank of the Raidak. However, there are many other villages with native Muslim populations (mainly converts from the Koch and Rajbanshi communities) from Alipurduar district of West Bengal to Kurigram district of Bangladesh. These native Muslims, also called Rajbanshi Muslims, are culturally and linguistically similar to Hindu Rajbanshis. However, their Islamic traditions have had a considerable impact on their culture and on the region as a whole. In the Bangladeshi part of the Raidak or Dudhkumar (mainly under Bhurungamari subdistrict; total population: 1,97,070; Muslims: 1,93,636, Hindus: 3390, Buddhists: 10 and others: 34), the people identify mainly as Rajbanshi Muslims. In this part, the Muslims follow traditional Islamic culture but with certain localized traditions.

Continuity of Primordial Culture

Though the Koch rulers encouraged the growth of Hinduism and Vaishnavism in the precolonial period, they did not impose any restrictions on the tribal people of the Raidak basin, allowing them to maintain their primordial culture. Therefore, a section of the Koch, Mech and Rabha tribes of the Raidak basin still continue to observe traditional religious practices. The Rabhas and Koches worship a traditional male deity called Rishi (Mahakal) and a female deity known as Jog. Their priests, called *deoshi/deodhai/huji*, perform ritual in honour of these chief deities. *Deoshis* are assisted by *deories*. The Meches are followers of Bathouism, i.e. worship of Bathou (a chief male deity equivalent to Shiva). There are many other deities who are also worshiped by the above-mentioned communities. Two daughters of the chief male deity—Rishi/Bathou—are common among these groups. The Rabhas call them Rountak and Basek while to the Meches they are known as Alai Khungri and Bilai Khungri. Rountak is a synthesized form of the Hindu goddesses Kali and Lakshmi. The Meches worship a similar female deity called Mouthansri or Lakshmi. On the other hand, the Koches (Rajbanshis) have maintained their tribal traditions (with a few modified aspects) in their religious practices and beliefs. The festivals of the Koch-Rajbanshis, such as Gocharbona (first plantation of paddy), Lakhi Dak (call to Lakshmi), Hudum Deo [call to the rain god], Mechini Khela (worship of river), Saleswari Puja (worship of forest god), etc., indicate that there is a close relationship between folk festivals and their lives. The Koch-Rajbanshis also observe a few other festivals such as Baishakhi, Ashadi Seva, Madan Kama, Gorakhnath, Bisua, Siyal Puja, Bishahari, Naya Khai, Jiga Thakur, etc., which are equally related to their livelihoods.

Synthesis of Culture

The growth of different religious cultures in the Raidak basin had an inexorable impact on its indigenous people. Based on the emergence of varied religious traditions, the synthesis of different cultures was almost unavoidable. The synthesis of religious culture has been observed in the worship of the chief male and female deities, i.e. Shiva and Shakti (Durga/Chandi/Gauri). Bhandani or Vanadevi (a tribal female deity) became a localized incarnation of Durga that is generally worshipped in the Raidak basin immediately after the immersion of Durga. The Rajbanshis of Paschim Nararthali, Madhya Nararthali, and Dakshin Nararthali have maintained the tradition of worshipping Bhandani with great enthusiasm.

Concurrently, a female tribal deity called Debi, is still worshipped by the ruling family of Cooch Behar in a synthesized form; Debi is a synthesis of both Durga and the chief female deity of the tribal communities. In this tradition, while rituals are generally performed by Kamrupi brahmins, the sacrifice of animals like tortoises and boars illustrate the strong influence of tribal religious concepts.

It has been already mentioned that Shiva or Mahakal is the chief male deity of both tribals and the non-tribals in the Raidak basin. Thus, Shiva is worshipped both by brahmins and tribal priests according to their respective traditions. The Koch Kingdom built several Shiva temples and employed *deories* to assist the brahmin priests of the temples. The tribal rituals relating to the deity are generally performed by these *deories*. The style of Shiva worship in the temples of

Bara Mahadeva at Baro Kodali, Chhoto Mahadeva at Nakkatigach, Mahakal of Mahakalguri village and many other Shiva temples of the region still bear the testimony of cultural synthesis. Moreover, certain tribal male deities, like Masan, Jakha, Bura Thakur, Dhum Baba, etc., are worshipped as Shiva; here, tribal traditions have a significant and impactful presence. During my fieldwork I also noticed the synthesis of Vaishnavism and Shaivism in the Raidak basin, where the two deities were worshipped in the same temple, e.g. in the Haribari and Shibbari temples of Kamakshyaguri.

Beside Shiva, Durga and Vishnu, specimens of religious synthesis are also available in certain other folk festivals and worship of folk deity. The Satyapida and the Paglapida are the synthesized form of the Hindu and the Islamic faiths. Most popular aspect of the Koch-Rajbanshi beliefs, however, is Garam puja where deities of the Hindu pantheon, Islamic faith and tribal concept of spirits have their equal presence.

Linguistic Diversity of the Raidak Basin

Language is the heart of any community, region, or nation. From Bhutan to Bangladesh, the areas along the two Raidaks have experienced the origin and evolution of different regional and national languages. The people of the Raidak basin in India depict wide variations in terms of their linguistics features. Several linguistic communities have settled in the Raidak I–Dhowlajhora–Raidak II basin. Among them, the Nepalese, the Meches (Bodos), the Rabhas, etc. are native people to this region. However, the labourers in the tea gardens hail from different linguistics groups, including the Santali, the Mundari, the Malpaharias, etc. The introduction of their local languages to the regions led to the growth of a common *lingua franca*, Sadri, in the tea gardens of the Duars. Sadri is now gradually emerging as an acceptable dialect in the Duars region including the Raidak basin.

On the other hand, since the 1930s, the Meches of the Raidak basin have shown an interest in the growth of their language and literature. The All Bodo Student Union (ABSU) and Bodo Sahitya Sabha of Assam have had considerable influence on the Meches of Alipurduar district. In fact, an Annual National Conference of the Bodo Sahitya Sabha was held in the Raidak basin (in Mahakalguri Mission High School) in 1984.[21]

Like the Meches, the Nepalese of the Raidak basin are also interested in cultivating their mother tongue, i.e. Nepali. Since the 1980s, they have supported the demand for the recognition of Nepali as a constitutional language of India. The celebration of poet Bhanubhakta Acharya's (1814–68) birthday or 'Bhanu Jayanti' has been a cultural marker for the Nepalese in the Raidak basin.

The Rabhas, except for those in the Chipra Beat, on the other hand, have remained isolated from their linguistic consciousness. However, the Rabhas of Dakshin Kamakshyaguri (in Alipurduar district) and Chengtimari, Nagururhaat, and Haripur villages (between the Raidak I and the Raidak II in Tufanganj subdivision) have experienced better linguistic progress. They have began codifying their folktales, memories and songs in their ownlanguage, known as

Kocha Krow. On the other hand, the Rabhas, Meches, Nepalese, Rajbanshis and other native communities have been greatly affected by the linguistics features of the East Bengali migrants after 1947. The East Bengalis have considerable influence on the linguistic domain of the native people of the Raidak basin. The indigenous communities of this region now use the East Bengali dialects in nearby markets while conversing with people of East Bengali origin.

However, the main linguistic issue of the Raidak basin relates to the status of the Kamtapuri/Rajbanshi language. The Rajbanshis, both Hindu (Scheduled Castes) and Muslim (Naishya Shaikhs or OBC-A) developed a consciousness of their 'mother tongue'. The Koch-Rajbanshi linguistic issue has a long history. It is associated with the formation of the Koch Kingdom. The Koch kings, like their contemporary tribal polities in North-East India, had adopted a convenient Indo-Aryan language that was widely accepted by speakers in eastern India, i.e. Bengali. This gradually became the official language of this kingdom. It was, however, not confined to the administrative levels. Rather, it was closely linked with the newly adopted religious culture. The linguistic issue of the Koch-Rajbanshis became a matter of concern in the late colonial period. Though educated Rajbanshis of northern Bengal and lower Assam first showed an interest in the upward social mobility of their fellow caste members, they eventually took an interest on the question of their language too. Panchanan Barma (1866–1935), the father of the Rajbanshi caste movement, not only wrote articles, poetry, and stories in the Rajbanshi language but also inspired his community to devote efforts towards the advancement of their own mother tongue. Since the 1960s, the Rajbanshis have founded several political and cultural organizations such as the Uttrakhanda Dal (UKD, 1969), the Bharatiya Koch-Rajbanshi Kshatriya Mahasabha (BKRM, 1984), the Koch-Rajbanshi International (KRI, 1986), the Bharatiya Kamata Rajya Parishad (BKRP, 1985), the Uttarbanga Tapasili Jati O Adibashi Samity (UTJAS, 1979), the Kamtapur Peoples' Party (KPP, 1995), and the Greater Cooch Behar Peoples' Association (GCBPA,1998). These organizations have always favoured the recognition of Rajbanshi/ Kamtapuri as a distinct language. The Rajbanshis have even utilized this linguistic issue as a primary factor for the demand of a 'separate province' in the northern part of West Bengal called 'Kamtapur or Uttarakhand'. In this context, Kumargram CD Block, Tufanganj and Boxirhat towns (along the course of the Raidak) contributed considerably towards the development of a 'sense of Rajbanshi belonging'. The UTJAS movement of the 1980s and the compilation and circulation of Kamtapuri/ Rajbanshi grammar and literary works from Tufanganj have drawn the attention of scholars.[22]

However, in the Bangladeshi part of the Raidak/ Dudhkumar basin, the Bengali language (*Bangla bhasha*) is the main factor for the integration of people into a 'national community'—Bangladeshis. From the language movement of 1952 to the present day, the Bengali language has been a driving force of national integrity for the people of the Dudhkumar basin.

Concluding Observations

Interactions between human beings and rivers are as old as human civilizations! In fact, since the beginning of the settled human civilization, rivers have been meeting the needs of the people living in their basins. In the academic field, rivers are not only being considered in the context of economic, ecological and strategic considerations, they are considered equally significant for cultural manifestations. Across the world, several rivers have been personified as mothers, sacred beings, hosts, and patrons as well as considered symbolic of regional cultures. In the context of the Raidak, all these features are notably present.

The Bhutanese part of the Raidak, called the Wang Chhu, is a symbol of the state's national culture, language, and identity. On the other hand, the Indian part of the Raidak basin has a close relationship with the growth of a pluralistic regional culture. This cultural pluralism, with a tradition of synthesis, is truly representative of the essence of Indian culture and heritage. Similar cultural trends are evident along the Bangladeshi course of the Raidak-Dudhkumar. So the Raidak is not only an ordinary river. The Raidak is truly a transnational river that helps us understand the cultural relations between a river and its people!

Notes

1. *Chhu* means river in Dzongkha, the national language of Bhutan.
2. For details, see Sangay Dorji, *The Biography of Zhabdrung Ngawang Namgyal, Pal Drukpa Rinpoche*, Thimpu: KMT Publication, 2008.

3. For details, see Rup Kumar Barman, *The Origin and Evolution of the Enclaves of India and Bangladesh: A Historical Study*, New Delhi: Abhijeet Publications; 2019, pp. 149–252.
4. There are a few Rabha villages outside the forest. The main villages of Alipurduar district are: (a) Chhipra Beat Rabha Basti, (b) Kodal Basti, (c) Poro Rabha Basti, and (d) Dakshin Kamakshyaguri. The Rabha villages of Cooch Behar district are: (a) Chengtimari, (b) Bochamari, (c) Nagururihaat, (d) Shalbari, and (e) Boxirhat.
5. The tribal communities of Chhotonagpur region (including the Santals, Mundas, Khariyas, Malpaharias, Birhors, Mahalis, Asuras, etc.) after migrating and settling in the Duars region of Jalpaiguri and Alipurduar districts of West Bengal have emerged as a united community. They are called the 'Madasias' by the natives as well as the non-tribal migrants of the Duars region.
6. The Gangadhar is an important river and originates in the Indo-Bhutan border near Buxa Fort. This hill stream flows here as the Jayanti River, descends into the plains of Alipurduar II CD Block, and then passes through Salsalabari, where it is called the Gangadhar. The Gangadhar flows through Bhatibari (in Alipurduar) and Natabari (in Cooch Behar district) and crosses the NH 31A near Ghogarkuti village. This river eventually meets the Raidak at Balabhut.
7. There is an extended tract of the Dudhkumar's riverbed on its right bank, called 'Chhit Tilai'. Chhit Tilai was recorded as a *chhitmahal* (enclave) of Bangladesh (as part of its Bhurungamari *upajela* or subdistrict) without population. It was officially transferred to India in 2015 by the Land Boundary Agreement (2015). For further details, see Rup Kumar Barman, *The Origin and Evolution of the Enclaves of India and*

Bangladesh, New Delhi: Abhijeet Publications, 2019, pp. 148–252.

8. *Kalika Puranam*, ed. Acharya Panchanan Tarkaratna, Calcutta: Naba Bharat Publishers, 1384 BS, Chapter 38, verses 95–101, p. 318 and Chapter 77, verses 30–2, p. 787.
9. *Yogini Tantra*, part I, ed. and tr. Swami Sarbeswarananda, Calcutta: Naba Bharat Publishers, 1385 BS, Chapter 13, verses 47–67, pp. 128–30.
10. T.W. Thomas Watters, *On Yuan Chwang's Travels in India (A.D. 629–645)*, vol. II, ed. Rhys Davids, S.W. Bhushel and Vincent Smith, Delhi, Munshiram Manoharlal, 1961, p. 186.
11. Minhas-ud-din Shiraj, *Tabakat-i-Nasiri*, tr. H.G. Raverty, New Delhi: Orient Books, 1970, p. 560.
12. The Kamakshya Temple inscription (originally inscribed in Sanskrit) says: 'Glory to the King Malla Deva, who by virtue of his mercy, is kind to the people, who in archery is like Arjun, and in charity like Dadhicchi and Karna; he is like an ocean of all goodness, and he is well-versed in many *sastras*; his character is excellent in beauty, he is as bright as Kandarpa, he is a worshiper of Kamakshya. His younger brother Sukladeva built this temple of bright stones on the Nila Hillock, for the worship of the Goddess Durga, in 1487 *Saka*. His beloved brother Sukladhvaja again, with universal fame, the crown of the greatest heroes, who, like the fabulous Kalpataru; gave all that was devotee asked of him, the chief of all devotees of the Goddess; constructed this beautiful temple with heaps of the stones on the Nila Hill in the 1487 *Saka*.' Per official records, the Kamakshya Temple had around 23,685 bighas of rent-free land for its maintenance. See Rup Kumar Barman, *From Tribalism to State: Reflections on the Emergence of the Koch Kingdom*, Delhi: Abhijeet Publications, 2007, p. 219.

13. Although there are several opinions about the characteristics of the Bhuiyans, it has generally been accepted that they were landed aristocrats. They developed advanced techniques and technologies for agricultural production and had considerable military power. The forefather of Sankaradev, Shiromony Bhuiyan, was the leaders of the Bhuiyans. The Charita Puthis have clearly constructed a history of conflict between the Ahom king and the Bhuiyans of the upper Brahmaputra valley.
14. Some of the officials of the royal court had embraced Vaishnavism which accelerated its spread in the Koch Kingdom. See Ramcharan Thakur, *Guru Charita*, 10th edn., Guwahati: Dutta Barua Publishing, 2001, verse 3454, p. 687.
15. Ibid., verses 3449–3453, pp. 686–7, verse 3606, p. 719 and verses 3729–33, p. 743.
16. For details about the satras of Assam and north Bengal, see S.N. Sharma, *The New Vaishnavite Movement and the Satra Institutions of Assam*, Gauhati: Gauhati University, 1966; Barman, *From Tribalism to State*, pp. 171–2, 218.
17. Dwijendra Nath Bhakat, *Satrar Samikshyattak Itibritta*, Dhubri: Bhabani Book House, 1995, p. 23.
18. Ibid., pp. 123, 145.
19. Fieldwork at Mahakalguri in October 2019.
20. For details see Minhas-ud-din Shiraj, *Tabaqat-i-Nashiri*.
21. From the days of the Brahma movement among the Bodos of lower Assam (1920–47), the Meches have always showed an interest in the growth of Bodo literature. Kalicharan Brahma, Rupnath Brahma, and many other thinkers have played a significant role in its growth. The Bodo Sahitya Sabha was founded in 1952 by the Bodo intellectuals of Assam along with

the Bodos of West Bengal, Meghalaya, and other states of North-East India.

22. During our fieldwork, we collected several works of notable scholars who were writing from Tufanganj. Among them we must mention the names of Dharma Narayan Barma, Ramendra Nath Adhikary, and Binod Bihari Barma.

Conclusion

The growth of civilizations along river basins has been a universal phenomenon since the prehistoric period. As natural resources, rivers have formed close relationships with the people living in their basins. But changes in river systems, either due to natural factors or human intervention, have an inevitable impact on the people who are dependent on them. In the present study I have mentioned how the Malo fishermen of East Bengal were forced to migrate from the Titash basin due to the rise of river's silt bed. Adwaita Malla Barman's novel *A River Called Titash* has categorically illustrated this phenomenon.

However, fishermen are not the sole dwellers of river basins. In fact, these regions are full of people with diverse occupations. The present study has observed that the Tista and the Brahmaputra basins offer true examples of pluralistic cultures in the Indian subcontinent. Debesh Roy and Jitendra Das have illustrated that the lifestyles of the indigenous people of the Tista and the Kalahi basins have been threatened due to colonial intervention in the natural resources of north Bengal and Assam. In the postcolonial period, the inevitable outcome of this interferences was manifested in the grievances of the natives of these regions in the form of movements for political autonomy and expulsion of outsiders. The Bideshi Kheda (Expulsion of Foreigners) phenomenon of the Assam Movement and the Bhatia Khedao (Expel the East Bengali Migrants) feature of the Uttar Khanda Movement in the late twentieth century have been thus represented in this work by two novels: *Kalahi Nadi: Ikul Hikul* and *Tista Parer Brittanta*.

Cultural changes and synthesis are two other characteristics of note in the river systems of South Asian countries. In the context of the Raidak River, the third chapter presents the Raidak (as the Wang Chhu) as a symbol of the national culture of Bhutan. The Bhutanese form of Buddhism and its national language Dzongkha have a profound relationship with the river. On the other hand, the Raidak basin has experienced the growth of a mixed culture along its Indian and Bangladeshi courses. The people of the Raidak basin in the two countries practise Hinduism, Vaishnavism, Islam, Christianity, indigenous faiths, as well as a host of cultural and religious traditions that incorporate aspects of all the aforementioned religions.

As a whole, the present study has found that the occupations, identity, politics, and culture of the dwellers of a particular river basin are closely allied, in many ways, with their rivers!

Bibliography

Works in Assamese

Bhakat, Dwijendra Nath, *Satrar Samikshyattak Itibritta*, Dhubri: Bhabani Book House, 1995.

Das, Jitendra, *Kalahi Nadi: Ikul Hikul*, Guwahati: Chandra Prakash, 1989.

Thakur, Ramcharan, *Guru Charita*, 10th edn., Guwahati: Dutta Barua Publishing, 2001.

Works in Bengali

Barman, Rup Kumar and Krishna Kumar Sarkar, eds., *Malo Jatir Itihas O Akar Grantha*, Kolkata: Cognition Publications, 2020.

Dakua, Dinesh, *Kamtapuri Andolon Ekti Jana Bichhinna Andolan*, Calcutta: National Book Agency, 2003.

Malla Barman, Adwaita, *Titash Ekti Nadir Naam*, tr. Kalpana Bardhan, New Delhi: Penguin, 1992.

———, *Adwaita Malla Barman Rachana Samagra*, ed. Achintya Biswas, Kolkata: Dey's Publishing, 2000.

Malla Barman, Mahendra Nath, *Jhalla Malla Parichary*, Mymensingh: Sen Brothers Press, 1914.

Roy, Debes, *Tistaparer Brittanta*, 16th edn., Kolkata: Dey's Publishing, 2013.

Works in English

Bandyopadhaya, D., 'Land Reforms in West Bengal: Remembering Harekrishna Konar and Benoy Choudhury', *Economic and Political Weekly*, vol. XXXV, no. 21, 2000.

Barman, Rup Kumar, *Migration, State Polices and Citizenship*, New Delhi: Aayu Publications, 2020.

———, *Caste, Class and Culture: The Malos, Adwaita Malla Barman and History of India and Bangladesh*, New Delhi: Abhijeet Publications, 2020.

———, *Fisheries and Fishermen: A Socio-economic History of Fisheries and Fishermen of Colonial Bengal and Post-colonial West Bengal*, Delhi: Abhijeet Publications, 2008.

———, *The Origin and Evolution of the Enclaves of India and Bangladesh: A Historical Study*, New Delhi: Abhijeet Publications, 2019.

———, *From Tribalism to State: Reflections on the Emergence of the Koch Kingdom*, New Delhi: Abhijeet Publications, 2007.

Bilsborrow, Richard and Pamela F. DeLargy, *Land Use, Migration and Natural Resource Deterioration: The Experience of Guatemala and Sudan*, Chapel Hill: The University of North Carolina, 1991.

Dorji, Sangay, *The Biography of Zhabdrung Ngawang Namgyal, Pal Drukpa Rinpoche,* Thimpu: KMT Publications, 2008.

El-Hinnawi, Essam, *Environmental Refugees,* Nairobi: United Nations Environmental Programme, 1985.

Equity and Justice Working Group Bangladesh, *Climate Change Induced Forced Migrants: In Need of Dignified Recognition under a New Protocol*, Dhaka: Equity BD, 2009.

Government of West Bengal, *Hataman Jara Tulechhe Shir (Bengali)*, Calcutta, Department of SC and ST, 1987.

Montgomery, Martin, *The History, Antiquities, Topography and Statistics of Eastern India*, 5 vols., 1838; repr., Delhi: Cosmo Publications, 1976.

Memorandum Submitted to the Scheduled Caste and Scheduled Tribe Commission by the Cooch Behar District Depressed Classes League, dated 29th April, 1961, Cooch Behar: Cooch Behar Depressed Classes League, 1961.

Proceedings of the First Annual Conference of the Siliguri Zonal Kshatriya Samity, dated 8th April, 1955, Siliguri: Siliguri Kshatriya Samiti, 1955.

Risley, H.H., *The Tribes and Castes of Bengal*, vol. II, Calcutta: Firma Mukhopadhyay, 1981.

Sharma, S.N., *The New Vaishnavite Movement and the Satra Institutions of Assam*, Gauhati: Gauhati University, 1966.

Shiraj, Minhas-ud-din, *Tabakat-i-Nasiri*, tr. H.G. Raverty, New Delhi: Orient Books, 1970.

Watters, T.W. Thomas, *On Yuan Chwang's Travels in India (A.D. 629–645)*, 2 vols., ed. Rhys Davids, S.W. Bhushel and Vincent Smith, Delhi: Munshiram Manoharlal, 1961.

Wise, James, *Notes on Race, Castes and Trades of Eastern Bengal*, London: Harrison and Sons, 1883.

Works in Sanskrit

Kalika Puranam, ed. Acharya Panchanan Tarkaratna, Calcutta: Naba Bharat Publishers, 1384 BS.

Yogini Tantra, ed. and tr. Swami Sarbeswarananda, Calcutta: Naba Bharat Publishers, 1385 BS.

Index

www.ingramcontent.com/pod-product-compliance
Lightning Source LLC
La Vergne TN
LVHW041113150826
845673LV00007B/2029